CELEBRATING OUR HERITAGE

Traditional Native American Arts and Activities

Arlette N. Braman

Illustrated by Bill Helin

John Wiley & Sons, Inc.

New York ■ Chichester ■ Weinheim ■ Brisbane ■ Singapore ■ Toronto

For Jean Ross, Comanche and Wichita, my first contact, who helped me get
started, and for David Michael Wolfe, Echota Cherokee tribe of
Alabama, who was willing to help without hesitation and
who checked my work throughout this project

Published by John Wiley & Sons, Inc.
Published simultaneously in Canada

Design and production by Navta Associates, Inc.

The publisher and the author have made every reasonable effort to ensure that the experiments and activities in this book are safe when conducted as instructed but assume no responsibility for any damage caused or sustained while
performing the experiments or activities in the book. Parents, guardians, and/or teachers should supervise young readers who undertake the experiments and activities in this book.

Library of Congress Cataloging-in-Publication Data:
Braman, Arlette N.
    Traditional Native American arts and activities / Arlette N. Braman.
        p. cm—(Celebrating our heritage)
    ISBN 0-471-35992-0 (pbk.)
        1. Indians of North America—Material culture—Juvenile literature. 2. Indian
craft—North America—Juvenile literature. I. Title. II. Series.

E98.M34 B73 2000
745'.087'97—dc21   00-043295

Printed in the United States of America

10 9 8 7 6 5 4 3 2 1

Contents

Acknowledgments

I am grateful to the many wonderful people who met with me and willingly shared information about their heritage: Amos Goodfox, Osage and Pawnee, Education Program Specialist, Department of Indian Education, Washington, D.C., for teaching me finger weaving, and Janet Goodfox, Osage, Budget and Accounting Analyst, Indian Health Service, Rockville, Maryland, for sharing her traditional ribbon work; Lettie Nave, Navajo, president of the Tsaile/Wheatfields chapter, who was so willing to help from the first time I called and introduced myself, and her husband, Flemen, for guiding me through the reservation; Terrol Johnson, Tohono O'odham, Tohono O'odham Basketweavers Organization, for sharing his exquisite basket weaving; Noreen Simplicio, Zuni, for showing me how she makes her beautiful pottery; Pauline Allred, Osage, for spending hours with me at the Osage Tribal Museum; Robin Hernandez and Pollyanna Nordstrand, Hopi, of the AH-TAH-THI-KI Museum, for teaching me about Seminole patchwork techniques; Roberta Jones, Seneca, for enlightening me about the Iroquois; and Barbara Free Spirit Shupe, Oglala Lakota, for praising my first attempts at beadwork.

Special thanks to the people who agreed to be featured in "The Tradition Continues" sections of the book: Peter B. Jones, Onondaga potter; Henry Washburn, Euchee elder; Janet Goodfox, Osage ribbon-work artist; Barbara Yazzie, Navajo rug weaver; Kevin Peters, Nez Perce flute maker; Clarissa Hudson, Tlingit artist; and Mattie Jo Aklacheak Ahgeak, Inupiat student.

A big thanks to all the local people who allowed me to interview them and shared so much with me about their worlds: Ed Calls Him, Eagle clan, Ponca Lakota; Keeto Big Mountain, Comanche and Apache; Daryl Thundercloud, Winnebago; and Pat Running Bear, Lenape and Cherokee.

I wasn't able to meet everyone in person, but the following people were extremely helpful with information through email and phone contact, by answering my questionnaires, checking my work, or by referring me to someone who could help: Dr. Patricia R. Wickman, Ph.D., director of the Department of Anthropology and Genealogy for the Seminole tribe of Florida; Jim Rementer, Lenape, language director for the Delaware tribe in the Lenape Language Preservation Program; Sandra Reinhardt of the Catawba Cultural Preservation Project; Dr. Wenonah Haire, Catawba, executive director,

Catawba Cultural Preservation Project; Mitchell Bush, Bear clan, Onondaga, editor of the American Indian Society newsletter; Tom Kennedy, director of the A:shiwi A:wan Museum and Heritage Center, Zuni, New Mexico; Linda C. Manuel Laubner, Tohono O'odham and Hia-ced O'odham; Bill Helin, Tsimshian artist and wood carver; Lionel deMontigny, Chippewa Cree; Jennie Mae Terrapin, Cherokee, manager of History and Culture at the Tsa-La-Gi Cultural Center, Tahlequah, Oklahoma; Lisa LaRue Tennison, Cherokee, Literature Review Coordinator, Cultural Resource Center, Cherokee Nation; David Michael Wolfe, Cherokee artist, writer, and historian; Josiah Blackeagle Pinkham, Nez Perce, ethnographer for the Cultural Resources Program of the Nez Perce tribe; Candace Lee Elknation, Miniconjou Lakota; Viola Ann Riebe, Hoh, advocate of education for Native Americans; Dan Molina; Marci Molina; Kathy Ahgeak, Inupiat, teacher at Ipalook Elementary School, Barrow, Alaska, who really came through for me; Mae and James Ahgeak, Inupiat, for allowing me to feature their daughter in the book; Chicky Swanson, Inupiat; Toni Raye (Uyagun) Schaeffer, Inupiat; Red Seeberger, Inupiat; Fran Shugak, Yupik, proprietor of Fran's Beads and Native Crafts and a commercial salmon fisherman, for giving me permission to use her recipe; Fanny Parker, Yupik Eskimo teacher, Togiak School; Bing Santamour, Yupik; Joan Hamilton, Cupik, curator of the Yupiit Piciryarait Cultural Center and Museum, Bethel, Alaska; Dr. Robert S. Leopold, archivist, National Museum of Natural History, Washington, D.C.; Linda Agren, assistant curator of Anthropology, Santa Barbara (California) Museum of Natural History; Fred Collins, Chumash; John Anderson; Trevor Sutter, Cree; Guy Gugliotta of *The Washington Post*; Margaret Stish, professor, East Stroudsburg (Pennsylvania) University, who gave me two wonderful contacts; Pat Pinciotti, professor, East Stroudsburg University, for always helping me out in a pinch; Larry Kelly, for helping me search the Web; my sister, Michelle Lagos, for connecting me with the Seminole Tribe of Florida; my cousin Emil Signes, for sending out my email requests; my cousin Margie Henry, who suggested I contact Jean Ross; and my husband, Gary, for shooting many of the photos in the book.

Thanks again to my editor, Kate Bradford, who encourages me to dig deeper; assistant editor Diana Madrigal, who's always so willing to help; Sibylle Kazeroid, for a super production job; all the people at Wiley who worked on this book; and Jude Patterson, for another great copyediting job.

The following children deserve a huge thanks for testing the activities: Elizabeth Decker, Jill Decker, Callan Braman, and Abigail Braman.

Author's Note

When I began working on this book, I felt excited, but also nervous. The only way I could write a book about the indigenous people of North America was to visit and talk with native peoples. So I began my search on the Internet, by going to powwows, visiting museums, and calling people on the phone I'd never met, hoping some would talk with me. Almost every person I spoke with was gracious and interested in sharing information about his or her world. These people welcomed me into their homes on the reservations and communities I visited, taught me how to make crafts authentically, showed me pictures of their ancestors, shared their wonderful stories, checked my finished work for accuracy, and helped me learn something about a culture of which I knew very little. It has enriched my life in ways I never dreamed possible. I have a much deeper respect for the people who first lived on American soil and for the many contributions they made and continue to make in our society.

I don't claim to be an expert in indigenous cultures. My goal in writing this book was to present information with accuracy and integrity, and to help heighten the awareness of nonindigenous children about North America's first people.

Out of respect, I have not included any activities such as making masks, Kachina figures, sand paintings, or anything that might be considered sacred, as I did not want to trivialize these sacred symbols. For consistency, it was decided to use the term *Native American,* though I respect the preference of many native peoples for the term *American Indian.*

I
THE NORTHEAST

The Northeast region of North America stretches from the western shore of Lake Superior to the Atlantic Ocean and from parts of southern Canada to the coast of North Carolina. Since the area is so large and geographically diverse, it is impossible to describe a common lifestyle among the original native inhabitants. In the 1600s and 1700s, the area was dominated by peoples who spoke Iroquoian, Algonquian, and cEastern Souian, but the various tribes had distint customs.

In the Great Lakes region, the Ojibwa gathered wild rice from birchbark canoes and collected maple syrup, a common staple of the Northeastern diet. Coastal tribes, such as the Wampanoag, fished in the waters off what is now Massachusetts and Rhode Island. The forests provided building materials for longhouses and wigwams, and supplied the Micmac, Mahican, and others with excellent hunting opportunities. The people established villages most often near water and grew corn, beans, squash, and tobacco.

Some of the Northeastern **nations** (tribes or a federation of tribes) today include Iroquois, Micmac, Kikapoo, Shawnee, Menominee, Chippewa, Algonquian, and Nanticoke.

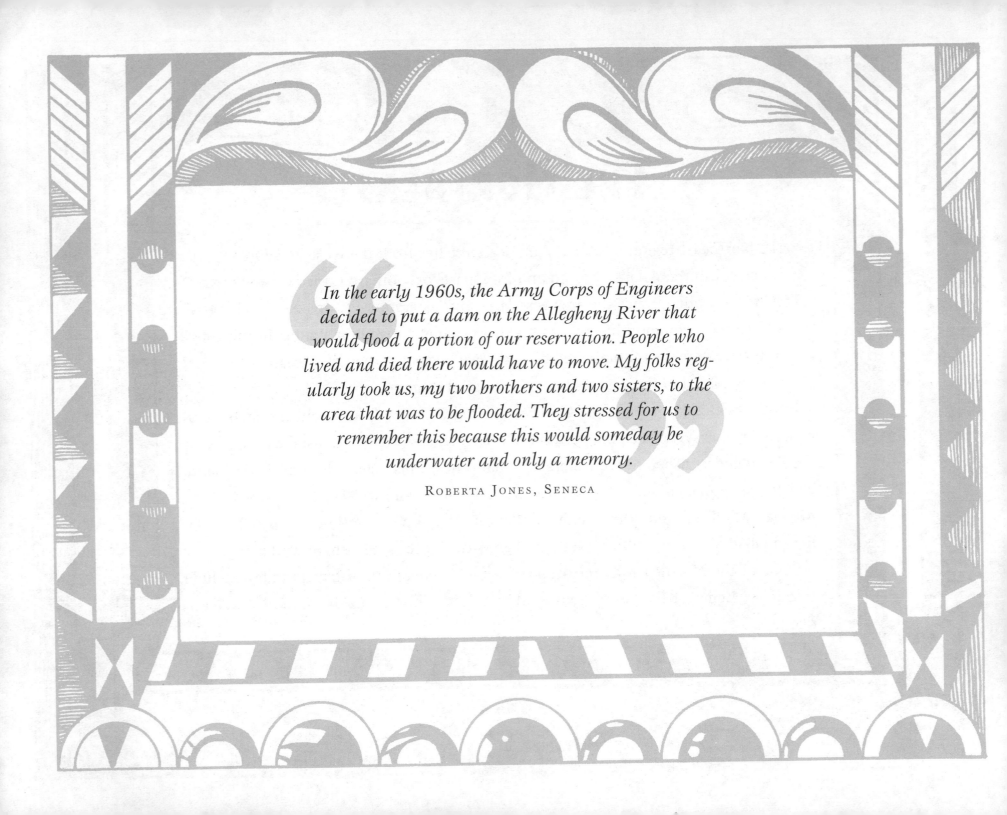

"In the early 1960s, the Army Corps of Engineers decided to put a dam on the Allegheny River that would flood a portion of our reservation. People who lived and died there would have to move. My folks regularly took us, my two brothers and two sisters, to the area that was to be flooded. They stressed for us to remember this because this would someday be underwater and only a memory."

ROBERTA JONES, SENECA

Winnebago Shoulder Bag

The Winnebago (win-uh-BAY-go) were skilled farmers who grew squash, corn, and beans on land north of the western shores of Lake Michigan in what is now Wisconsin. They traded their extra harvest for rice from their neighbors, the Menominee (meh-NAH-meh-nee). Sometimes they traveled to the Plains to hunt buffalo, trading many of the hides with other tribes or with European fur traders for things they needed. The surrounding forests provided them with bark for their wigwams.

WINNEBAGO TRADITION

The Winnebago are organized into **clans** (divisions or groups within a tribe that are closely related) and trace their descent and clan membership through their fathers. The two main divisions are the Upper (Sky) and the Lower (Earth). The Thunderbird is the most important Sky clan and the Bear is the most important Earth clan. Clan organization creates close family ties. Children call their father's sisters *noni* (NAH-nee), which means "Mom," and their father's brothers *jugi* (JUH-jee), which means "Dad." These aunts and uncles are considered as much moms and dads as the children's real moms and dads.

Today the Winnebago are divided into two groups. The Wisconsin Winnebago, who are now known by their original name, Ho-Chunk (HO-chunk), which means "Sacred Language" or "Master Language," live on some 4,400 acres (1,781 ha) of reservation land in Wisconsin, and the Nebraska Winnebago, who maintain this name, occupy some 27,500 acres (11,129 ha) there.

The Winnebago made pouches and shoulder bags from the skins of animals, such as otter and deer. They decorated these bags with beadwork and porcupine quills. After the Europeans arrived, the Winnebago traded skins for fabric, which they also used to make pouches and bags. They decorated the fabric bags with unique floral designs using needlework, **appliqué** (a cutout decoration attached or sewn to a larger piece of material for accent), or by sewing on tiny beads. Some bags were decorated with as many as 80,000 beads. Your Winnebago shoulder bag, decorated with traditional floral designs, will be made from felt.

THE RESERVATION

For centuries, the Winnebago had occupied land in northeast Wisconsin. From the mid-1600s until the late 1800s, the Winnebago were forced to relocate to Iowa, South Dakota, Minnesota, and Nebraska due to local wars, invasion by other nations, land settlement by European immigrants, and governmental dictates. Many kept returning to their original homeland, and finally the federal government purchased land in Wisconsin for those who wanted to remain. This land became known as a **reservation** (a tract of land set aside for use by a group of people).

Here's What You Need

- [ ] 6 felt pieces, 9 by 12 inches (23 by 30.5 cm), in a variety of colors
- [ ] ruler
- [ ] chalk
- [ ] scissors
- [ ] pencil
- [ ] white paper
- [ ] patterns from this book
- [ ] straight pins
- [ ] fabric glue
- [ ] needle
- [ ] thread
- [ ] self-adhesive Velcro

Here's What You Do

1 Select two felt pieces in any color. These pieces will be the front and the back of your bag. Measure a 9-by-9-inch (23-by-23-cm) square on whichever piece you want to be the front of the bag, and use the chalk to mark where you need to cut. Cut on the chalk mark. Do not cut the back piece. Set these two felt pieces aside.

2 For the handle, cut two 12-by-2-inch (30.5-by-5-cm) pieces from another piece of felt, in any color. Set these pieces aside.

3 Trace the leaf, the flower parts, and the parallelogram patterns in this book, using the pencil and white paper. Cut out the shapes.

4 Plan your bag's design using paper and pencil. Use the illustrations here as a guide to assemble the pieces in a floral design. Think about the colors you want to use for each piece in your design.

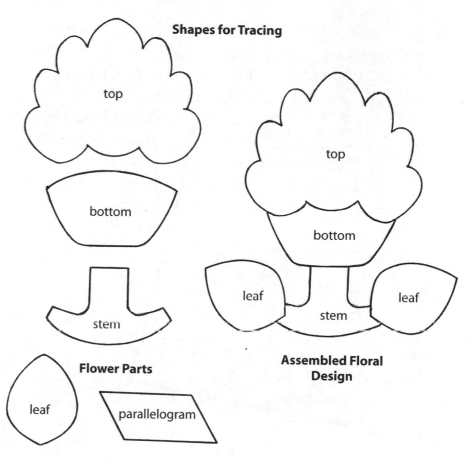

Shapes for Tracing

top

bottom

stem

leaf

Flower Parts

leaf

parallelogram

top

bottom

leaf

leaf

stem

Assembled Floral Design

5 Working with one cutout pattern piece at a time, lay it on the remaining felt, and hold or pin the pattern in place while tracing the shape with the chalk. Do this for each pattern piece. You will need about this many pieces of each shape: leaf—12, stem—2, bottom of flower—2, top of flower—2, parallelogram—6. Cut out the felt shapes and set them aside.

6 Take the 9-by-9-inch (23-by-23-cm) piece of felt you cut for the front of the bag, and lay it on your work surface. Arrange the cutout felt shapes on the front of the bag as shown. (Eight of the leaf shapes will be used later.) The top of the flower design should be about $2^3/_4$ inches (7 cm) down from the top edge of the front. Place the parallelograms in a zigzag along the bottom.

Place top of flower $2^3/_4$ inches (7 cm) down from top edge of front

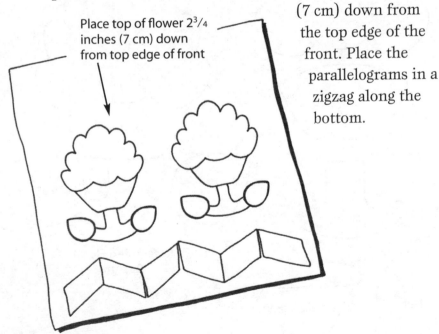

7 Glue the cutout shapes to the front of the bag, using the fabric glue. Press each piece firmly after gluing. Let the glue dry completely.

8 Take the two handle strips and pin them together along two of the short edges. Sew these strips together, leaving a $^1/_4$-inch (.5-cm) seam. Use a running stitch as shown.

Running Stitch

Leave $^1/_4$-inch (.5-cm) seam

Stick needle down and up through material and continue sewing in this way

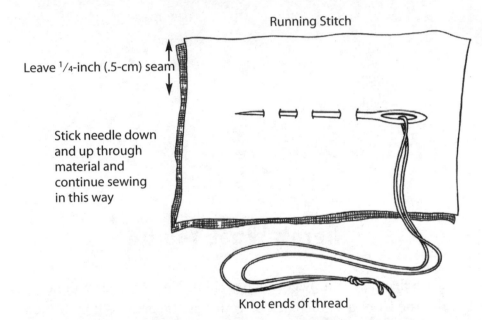

Knot ends of thread

9 Lay the sewn handle on your work surface so that the seam is facedown. Glue the remaining eight leaf shapes to the faceup side of the handle. The leaves should be spaced evenly and the leaves at each handle end should be 3 inches (7.5 cm) from the edge. Press the leaves firmly after gluing. Set the handle aside to dry completely.

10 Take the piece of felt you chose for the back of the bag, and lay it faceup on your work surface. When the leaves on the handle are dry, place the handle ends, with leaves facedown, on each side at the top of the back as shown. The area of the back above the handles will be the flap of your bag. The ends of the handle should be 7½ inches (19 cm) from the bottom of the back. Pin the handle ends in place. Sew the handle ends to the felt piece. Use a running stitch in a 1½-inch (4-cm) square pattern as shown. Sew neatly since your stitches will be visible.

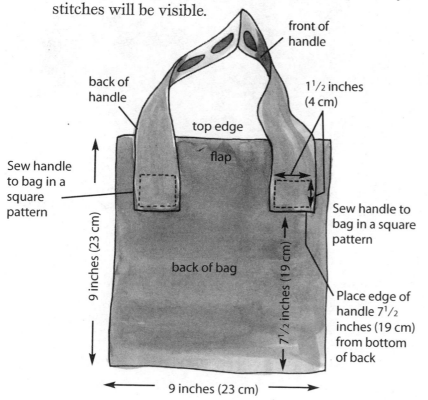

back of handle

front of handle

1½ inches (4 cm)

top edge

flap

back of bag

Sew handle to bag in a square pattern

Sew handle to bag in a square pattern

9 inches (23 cm)

7½ inches (19 cm)

Place edge of handle 7½ inches (19 cm) from bottom of back

9 inches (23 cm)

11 Turn the back of the bag over. Place the front of the bag, design faceup, on top of the back of the bag, *lining up the bottom edges.* (The handle should be behind the flap on the back of the bag.) Pin the front and back pieces of the bag together.
Starting at the top right edge, sew the front and back pieces together as shown. Use a running stitch and leave a ¼-inch (.5-cm) seam. Sew neatly since your stitches will be visible.

back of bag (flap)

front of bag

Pin front and back pieces together

Use a running stitch to sew front of bag to back, leaving a ¼-inch (.5-cm) seam

Line up bottom edges

12 Center one of the pieces of self-adhesive Velcro on the front of the bag about 1 inch (2.5 cm) from the top edge. Center the other piece of Velcro on the inside flap of the bag as shown. Your Winnebago bag is ready to use.

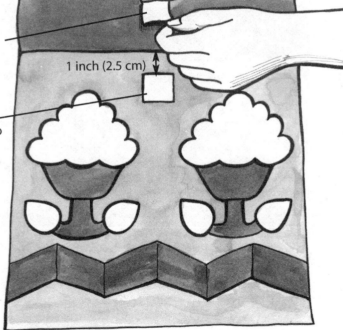

Center other piece of Velcro on inside flap

1 inch (2.5 cm)

Center self-adhesive Velcro 1 inch (2.5 cm) down from top edge of front

"You need to learn to work in society. . . . I still have my heritage. I don't let that go."

DARYL THUNDERCLOUD, WINNEBAGO

Lenape Grape Dumplings

The Lenape (len-AH-pay) made their home in what is now New Jersey, eastern Pennsylvania, northern Delaware, and southeastern New York. This land was called Lënapehòking (len-AH-pay-HAWK-ing), which means "Land of the Lenape." The Lenape, like all Native Americans, have always believed that all things on earth, such as animals, trees, insects, and air, have a spirit and should be respected. They hunted only what they needed, drying much of the catch for later use, and traveled the rivers in dugout canoes. Large groups of families lived in houses made from elm or chestnut bark. After many hours of work, families enjoyed spending the evenings together in storytelling. Oftentimes, the elders told myths and legends that explained the Lenape's beginnings.

LENAPE TRADITION

Storytelling continues to be an important part of all Native American life. Some native peoples believe that stories should be told only during certain seasons. The Lenape believe that some stories may be told all year long, but special stories called *at'hiluhakana* are told only in winter. If one of these stories is told at a time other than winter, the Lenape believe it is important to say, "I am seated on twelve skunk skins." This will keep away things such as bugs that will come after you for telling a story out of season.

Contact with Swannuken, or "Saltwater People," as the Lenape called them, began in the early 1500s when Giovanni da Verrazano, an Italian navigator, arrived in New York harbor. The Lenape were subjected to slave raids and diseases. Fur trading with Europeans led to competition and fighting among neighboring tribes. The Lenape were forced to move west to Ohio and Kansas. Eventually, many settled in Oklahoma. Today many Lenape live in Oklahoma, Kansas, Wisconsin, New Jersey, Pennsylvania, and Ontario, Canada. Lenape means "the People."

Lenape women were responsible for planting, harvesting, and preparing meals, which were eaten twice a day. Staples included corn, beans, and squash, which were combined with a variety of foods, such as potatoes, wild peas, an assortment of nuts, and many kinds of berries. A traditional dish, *shëwahsapan* (sha-wah-SAH-pahn), or grape dumplings, was part of many meals and was made with the juice of wild grapes that grew in the area. You can make this easy dish to enjoy whenever you want a taste of Lenape food.*

Here's What You Need

SERVINGS: ABOUT 6
Recipe requires adult help.

Ingredients
- 8 cups (2 liters) Concord grape juice
- 1 cup (240 ml) sugar
- 1½ cups (360 ml) flour
- ½ tablespoon (7.5 ml) butter, cut into small chunks
- ¾ cup (180 ml) Concord grape juice

Equipment
- measuring cup
- large pot
- mixing spoon
- food mixer with bowl
- rolling pin
- knife
- slotted spoon
- serving bowl
- aluminum foil

*Recipe by Nora Thompson Dean from *Touching Leaves Indian Crafts*, copyright 1991. Used with permission.

> *My oldest brother hewed a huge log about twenty feet long like a canoe. The trough was smooth and slick from the many years of the horses eating from it. It was so big sometimes I would lie down in it on cool summer evenings and watch the stars and meditate.*
> *It is easy to relive those long-ago days on the farm, as to me it seems like only last week.*
>
> NORA THOMPSON DEAN, "TOUCHING LEAVES WOMAN," LENAPE (1907–84)

Here's What You Do

1 Pour the 8 cups (2 liters) of grape juice and the sugar into the large pot and stir. Heat the mixture at medium to medium-high, stirring occasionally.

2 In the bowl of the electric mixer, mix the flour, butter, and the ¾ cup (180 ml) of grape juice. The texture should be somewhat firm and should hold together well. If you don't have a food mixer, mix by hand using the mixing spoon.

3 Divide the dough into two portions. Roll out each portion of dough on a clean, floured surface to about 12 inches (30.5 cm) in diameter and about ¼ inch (.5 cm) thick.

4 Cut strips from each circle about ¾ inch (2 cm) wide. Then cut the strips into 3-inch (7.5-cm)-long pieces. These pieces are your dumplings.

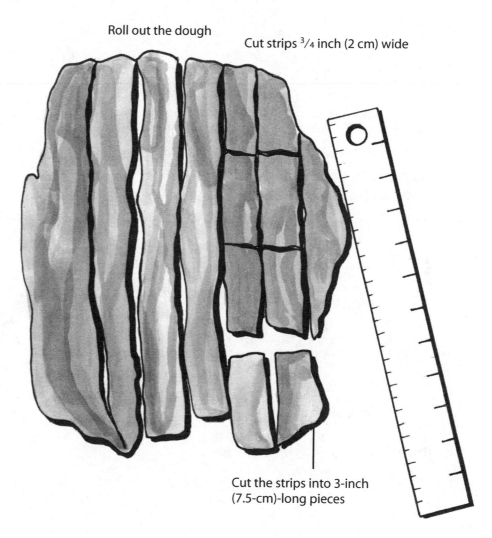

Roll out the dough

Cut strips ¾ inch (2 cm) wide

Cut the strips into 3-inch (7.5-cm)-long pieces

5 When the juice-and-sugar mixture is gently boiling, *ask an adult* to help you add the first batch of dumplings (about 15 to 20). They will float to the top almost immediately. Stir the dumplings and cook on a low boil for about 15 minutes. Adjust the heat if necessary. Use the slotted spoon to transfer the cooked dumplings to the serving bowl. Place a piece of aluminum foil over the bowl to keep the dumplings warm.

6 If the grape juice becomes too thick and syrupy, add some water. Cook the next batch of dumplings, then place them in the serving bowl. You can eat your grape dumplings as a side dish with your main meal.

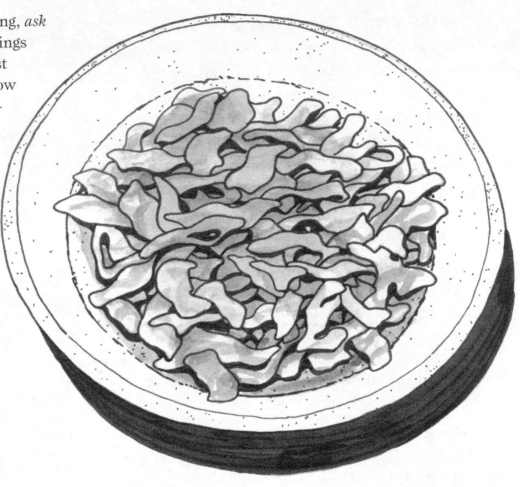

> *Even if you choose to appear still, in your place, [so as] not to change, change will appear in the place you choose to be.*
>
> PAT RUNNING BEAR,
> LENNI LENAPE NATION,
> BRIDGETON, NEW JERSEY

Iroquois Tree of Peace

The Iroquois (EAR-ih-kwoy) Confederacy is a group made up of six different nations of Native Americans, including Mohawk, Oneida, Onondaga, Cayuga, Seneca, and Tuscarora. Their ancestors came from the West and the South to settle in the Northeastern region of North America between A.D. 1200 and 1400. Some Iroquois tribes lived as far north as Canada, while others extended into the Carolinas. The people lived in longhouses, one of which could house up to 20 extended families. Corn was a main staple of the people and was grown with squash and many varieties of beans. These foods became known as the Three Sisters because the seeds of these foods were planted together and grew together in harmony. Women scattered sacred tobacco on the ground before harvesting any food, as a way of giving thanks to the plants for providing food.

The Iroquois were a resourceful people who hunted animals from the surrounding forests for food and fished the many rivers, lakes, and streams. The Iroquois always gave thanks by saying a prayer to the animal that gave of itself to provide food for the people. They used trees and bark to build their longhouses, to make masks used in ceremonies, and to make utensils, such as bowls, trays, and birch-bark baskets. Many Iroquois today continue to practice their traditional way of life.

THE IROQUOIS AND THE AMERICAN REVOLUTION

The Iroquois as a confederacy did not take part in the American Revolution (1775–83) but let each nation decide for itself whether to participate. At the close of the Revolutionary War, the Iroquois who had fought with the British were invited by the British to go to Ontario, Canada, to settle on land that had been set aside for them by the British, thereby creating two main Iroquois groups—one in Ontario and the other in New York.

In the 1790s, the Iroquois sold some of their land to New York, reserving the remaining land for themselves. They were able to resist permanent removal in 1830 when Congress passed the Indian Removal Act calling for the removal of Eastern tribes to land west of the Mississippi. Before signing any treaties, some Iroquois went to see if Kansas would be an acceptable alternative home. They decided it wasn't. The head chief of the confederacy, Abraham La Forte, informed the governor that they were not going to leave their homeland. Since New York lands were not federal lands, the governor of New York saw no reason for the Iroquois to move. Today many live on their lands in New York. Others live in Wisconsin, in cities and towns throughout the United States, and in Ontario and Quebec, Canada. The Iroquois call themselves Ö gwe` ö weh (on-GWIH-on-way), which means "Real People," and Haudenasaunee (ho-dee-no-SHO-nee), which means "Those of the Longhouse." (The Iroquois speak the same language, but there are some differences in dialects among the nations.)

IROQUOIS TRADITION

The Iroquois follow a clan system. Each nation has a different number of clans. The Onondaga have the Beaver, Turtle, Eel, Snipe, Heron, Bear, Wolf, and Deer clans. Clan ancestry is traced through the mother. For all the nations, each clan is headed by a clan mother and she chooses the man who will represent her clan on the council. She can remove him from the council if she feels he is not doing his job adequately.

Before the Iroquois became a confederacy in the mid-1500s, the different Northeastern nations often fought among themselves. A Huron holy man, Deganawidah, had a dream that he would bring a message of the Great Peace to the people. He enlisted the aid of Hiawatha, an Iroquois peacemaker, and together they spread the message to the people. Eventually, the Great Peace, consisting of peace, justice, sharing, and the equality of all life, became law. When the Iroquois nations agreed to live in peace, they buried their weapons beneath the Tree of Peace. The tree came to symbolize peace, and its roots grew in the four sacred directions—north, east, south, and west—stretching out to all who wished to find peace. From all directions, anyone could follow the roots back to the tree. An eagle sat on top of the tree as a watchful eye for danger. Your Tree of Peace will be a symbol of all the things you can do in your life to live in peace with all people and all things in nature.

Here's What You Need

- tree branch*
- ruler
- scissors
- 2 sheets of construction paper, 8½ by 11 inches (21.5 by 28 cm) each
- empty coffee can
- tape
- stones
- pencil
- yarn

*The Iroquois Tree of Peace is a white pine, so use a pine branch. If pine trees don't grow in your area, use another kind of branch.

Here's What You Do

1 Find a branch that has fallen from a tree in your backyard or in a park. *Do not break a branch off a tree.* The branch should measure about 2 feet (61 cm) long and have at least four limbs.

2 Cut a piece of construction paper to fit the coffee can and secure the paper to the can with tape. Place the end of the tree branch in the empty coffee can. While holding the branch, fill the coffee can three-fourths full with the stones. The stones will help your branch stand upright in the can.

3 Cut the second piece of construction paper into four equal pieces. On each piece of paper, write a peace message that you can live by each day. Here are some ideas: "I will accept people the way that they are"; "I will be kind to everyone"; "I will treat people the way that I like to be treated." With the pencil point, poke a small hole at the top of each message.

4 Cut four pieces of yarn, each about 8 inches (20 cm) long. Slip each yarn strand through each hole on the messages. Tie the ends of each yarn strand in a knot or bow, then hang each peace message on one of the limbs of the branch. Your Tree of Peace will remind you to live in peace with everyone.

"We see ourselves as a sharing society. We help each other. . . . My family was poor; we had to gather foods like leeks, cowslips, milkweeds, maple sap, and berries to supplement our meals. My mother always said that we were rich in our way of life and not to base the worth of a person by what's on the outside, but what's on the inside."

Mitchell Bush, Onondaga

THE TRADITION CONTINUES

PETER B. JONES, ONONDAGA POTTER

Over the past 25 years, the art of making Iroquois pottery in the traditional style has been revived. Unfortunately, there is no oral history about the techniques of ancient Iroquois pottery making. There are no living mentors from whom contemporary potters can learn. Because of this, it has been a challenge for artists like Peter B. Jones to find answers to the many questions about how his ancestors created these earthen containers.

As a contemporary artist, Peter B. Jones believes that by creating his unique style of pottery, he is able to connect to his roots. He uses local clay, mined clay, and manufactured clay to create his pottery. Because he makes so many pieces, he prefers manufactured clay, since local clay takes a great deal of time to prepare. Although today's Iroquois pottery is not used in the same way as it was long ago, it serves as a link to the pottery of the Iroquois ancestors.

> *I use both the coil method and modified slab method in hand-building pottery. My personal research of original pottery shards leads me to believe that both methods were used, depending on the design of the pot.*
>
> PETER B. JONES, ONONDAGA POTTER

II

THE SOUTHEAST

The Southeast region of North America covers an area from Tennessee to the Gulf of Mexico and from the East Coast to the Mississippi Valley. The landscape includes mountains, rivers, swamps, coastal areas, valleys, and woods. This diversity supported different lifestyles among the native peoples living in the region. Some, such as the Creek, were excellent farmers who raised corn, beans, and squash in the relatively mild climate in what is now Alabama and Georgia. The Choctaw hunted with bows and arrows and with blowguns made from river cane that grew in the abundant forests in present-day Mississippi and Alabama. The Seminole of Florida constructed canoes from which to fish and travel the rivers, establishing trade routes with other tribes. The many trees provided building materials for the villages that were established among all tribes. All of the Southeastern tribes lived off the land in a harmonious and respectful way. Some Southeast nations today include Choctaw, Chickasaw, Euchee, Cherokee, Muskogee, Apalachee, Seminole, Catawba, Shaponi, Mohetan, Monacan, and Powhatan.

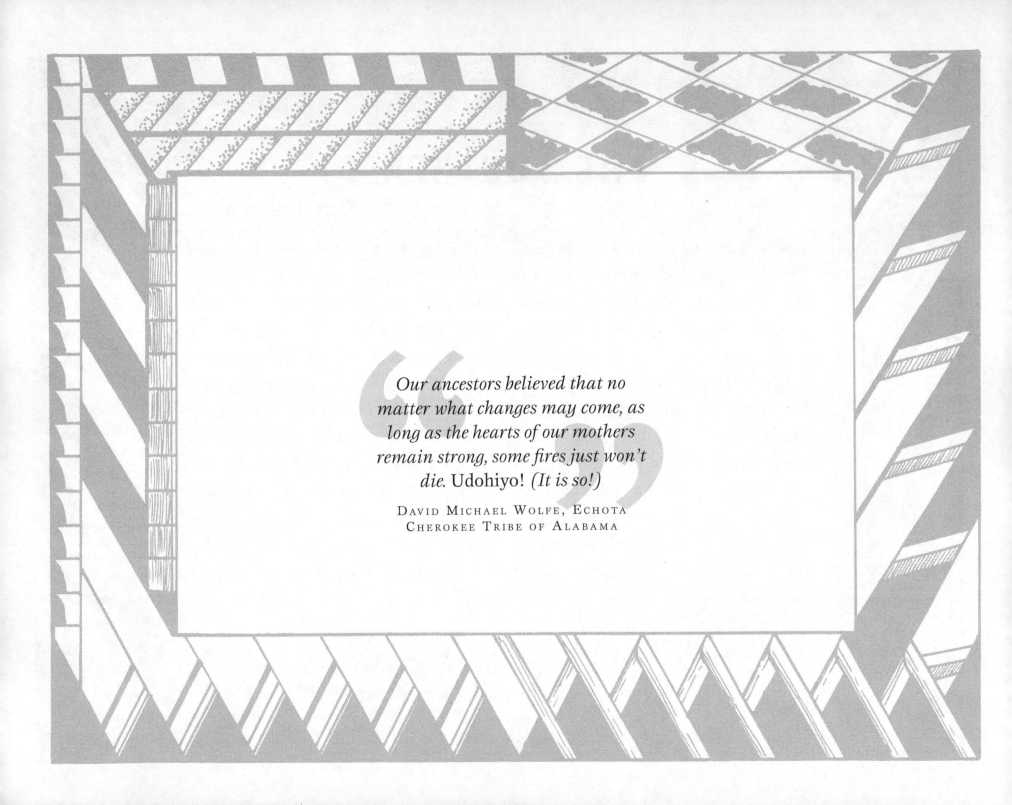

"*Our ancestors believed that no matter what changes may come, as long as the hearts of our mothers remain strong, some fires just won't die.* Udohiyo! (*It is so!*)"

DAVID MICHAEL WOLFE, ECHOTA
CHEROKEE TRIBE OF ALABAMA

Seminole Patchwork Coaster

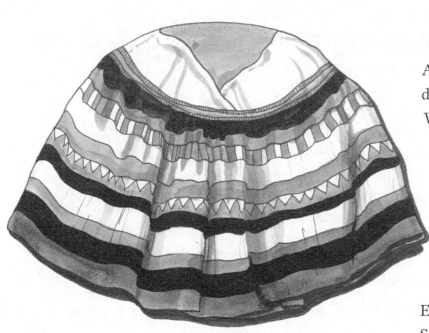

The ancestors of the modern tribal members of the Florida Seminole (SEM-uh-nohl) and Miccosukee (mihk-uh-SOO-kee) lived in a large area of the Southeast, in what is today Georgia, Alabama, and Florida, for at least 12,000 years. Consisting of many different tribes, they were known as the Maskókî (mosh-KOH-gih). When the Spaniards arrived in the early 1500s, and when other Europeans arrived in the 1600s, many Maskókî left their towns and cities and migrated southward rather than live under European control. Eventually, these diverse peoples came to be known as Seminole and Creek, names given to them by the English-speaking settlers. During the 1800s, when the government forced the removal of many native peoples to Indian Territory, a handful of people hid in the swamps known as the Everglades and survived. Today the descendants of the Maskókî, the Seminole and Miccosukee tribal members, continue to live on the land that hid their ancestors.

INDIAN TERRITORY

In 1829, the U.S. government set aside land in what is now Oklahoma and forced the removal of many Native Americans to this land. The land was called Indian Territory. Native Americans were told they would never have to leave this land. However, the territory was cut in half in 1890 and one part was named Oklahoma.

The Florida Seminole have citizens who speak Mikísuukî (mih-go-SOO-kee) and Maskókî. Most Mikísuukî-speaking Seminole live on reservations in Hollywood, Big Cypress, Immokalee, and Tampa. Most Florida Maskókî-speaking Seminole live on the Brighton reservation. The members of the Miccosukee tribe live along the Tamiami Trail, on special lands within the Everglades National Park, and on reservation lands that straddle Alligator Alley (Interstate 75).

The Seminole were skilled artisans in beadwork, basketry, **finger weaving** (weaving done without a loom, using only the fingers), and sewing men's long shirts and women's skirts, blouses, and capes from **calico** (cotton cloth with patterns) with patchwork for accent. Many continue these traditions today. But

it is their patchwork clothing for which they are most famous. Using the patchwork technique, you can make a **coaster** (a small mat used to protect a tabletop or other surface) with a simple design.

SEMINOLE TRADITION

Already experienced in sewing techniques, Seminole women, in the early 1900s, were experimenting with patchwork and creating eye-catching, multicolored designs by sewing together strips of cloth. This unique patchwork technique is still used by Seminole women today.

Here's What You Need

- [ ] scissors
- [ ] scraps of cotton material (turquoise, red, green, yellow, and purple)
- [ ] ruler
- [ ] pencil
- [ ] straight pins
- [ ] needle
- [ ] thread
- [ ] sewing machine (optional)
- [ ] iron (may require adult help)
- [ ] ironing board
- [ ] polyester fill*

*Use a thermal fill, as it will act as an insulator.

Here's What You Do

1 Cut two strips of material (one turquoise and one red), each measuring 9 by 1½ inches (23 by 4 cm). Use the pencil to mark your cut lines.

2 With right sides facing, pin the strips together on the long edges. Sew the strips together, either by hand using a running stitch (see page 6) or by machine. Leave a ¼-inch (.5-cm) seam.

3 After you finish sewing the strips together to make one piece, press the seam flat with the iron. *Ask an adult for help with the iron if you have never used one.*

4 Cut the piece you just sewed into rectangular strips, cutting across the seam. Make each strip 1½ inches (4 cm) wide. You will have six strips.

Cut 6 strips, each measuring 1½ inches (4 cm) wide

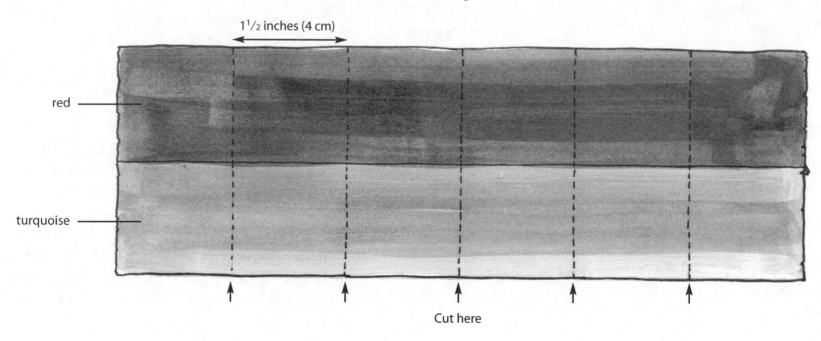

1½ inches (4 cm)

red

turquoise

Cut here

5 Lay the strips on your work surface in a checkerboard pattern with seams matching as shown. With right sides facing, pin the pieces together along the cut edges. Sew the strips together. Leave a ¼-inch (.5-cm) seam. Press the seams flat with the iron. Set this red-and-turquoise piece aside.

6 Cut six strips (two green, two yellow, and two purple), each measuring 6½ by 1½ inches (16.5 by 4 cm).

7 With right sides facing, pin one green strip to one yellow strip and sew them together, leaving a ¼-inch (.5-cm) seam. Pin the yellow strip of this piece to one purple strip and sew them together. Repeat this step with the remaining three strips, following the same color order, so that you have two identical pieces. Press the seams flat.

8 With right sides facing, pin the free edge of each purple strip to each side of the red-and-turquoise piece and sew these together. Press the seams flat. This piece is the front of the coaster.

With right sides facing and seams matching, sew strips together

seam   seam   seam   seam   seam

red   turquoise   red   turquoise   red   turquoise

Match seams →

turquoise   red   turquoise   red   turquoise   red

Sew strips together

9 Cut a piece of material, in any color, 8½ by 6½ inches (21.5 by 16.5 cm). This is the back of the coaster. Set this piece aside.

10 Cut a piece of polyester fill, 8¼ by 6¼ inches (21 by 16 cm). Sandwich the polyester fill and the coaster pieces together. To do this, lay the back piece of the coaster on your work surface, right side up. Lay the front piece of the coaster on the back piece, wrong side up. (The raw edges of the seams should be faceup.) Lay the polyester fill on top of the front piece. Pin all three pieces together. Starting at the top of one long edge, sew down this edge, across the bottom, and up the other long edge, leaving a ¼-inch (.5-cm) seam. Sew over your last stitch three times, then cut the thread.

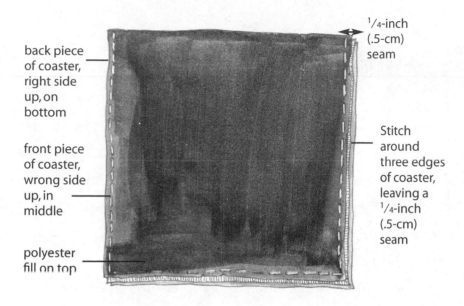

back piece of coaster, right side up, on bottom

front piece of coaster, wrong side up, in middle

polyester fill on top

¼-inch (.5-cm) seam

Stitch around three edges of coaster, leaving a ¼-inch (.5-cm) seam

11 Turn the coaster right side out, making sure the fill is between the front and back pieces. Iron the coaster so the outer edges lie flat.

12 Fold under ¼ inch (.5 cm) of the top, raw edges so they are tucked inside the coaster. Pin and sew the edges together. You can use the coaster under a cup of tea or a can of soda.

I learned to carve canoes from my uncles and my grandfather. I grew up so far south in Florida that there wasn't much land. It took us all day to pole the dugout canoe to the nearest trading post to trade our alligator hides for coffee, flour, and other things we needed.

HENRY JOHN BILLIE, ELDER AND MASTER CANOE CARVER, SEMINOLE TRIBE OF FLORIDA

Catawba Roasted Corn

The Catawba (cuh-TAW-buh) lived in what is now South Carolina's Piedmont region, where rolling hills create a beautiful landscape. Excellent soil conditions enabled the Catawba to farm the land. The surrounding woodlands created ideal hunting grounds for small animals, such as squirrels, rabbits, and birds, and the Catawba crafted blowguns for these small-prey hunts. They lived in villages of circular, bark-covered houses. Because of their location along the Catawba River, the Catawba developed a successful river trade that can be traced as far back as 2500 B.C. They excelled in pottery making and crafted sturdy cookware and ceremonial vessels that were much in demand with many tribes along the Catawba River. This art has never died out and potters today dig clay from the ground, prepare it, make the pots using a coiled technique, smooth the pots with rubbing stones, and fire the pottery using traditional methods.

CATAWBA TRADITION

The blowgun was an important tool used for hunting small animals and birds. Traditionally, blowguns were made from a cane tube or from swamp alder and were about 5 to 6 feet (1.5 to 2 m) long. The darts were made from pine, oak, or cedar pieces, with one end carved to a sharp point. Soft feathers were attached to the other end. Boys as young as 10 years old became experts at using the blowgun. When a hunter spotted his target, he placed the dart inside the blowgun and blew into the blowgun, shooting the dart into the animal.

First contact with Europeans may have been in the 1600s. Wars with neighboring tribes and the French drastically reduced the Catawba population, as did diseases, and land settlement by nonnatives forced the Catawba to lose much of their homelands. Today most of the nearly 2,500 Catawba live on a reservation in South Carolina and continue to maintain a strong belief in the traditions of their ancestors. The Catawba call themselves Ye Iswa (yang EES-wong), which means "River People."

The Catawba cultivated many foods, including corn, squash, potatoes, and beans. Corn has always been an essential food to many Native Americans and continues to be a part of many ceremonies. Roasted corn is a favorite food of the Catawba. A yummy way to prepare the corn is to grill it after it has soaked in water for an hour. The Catawba say that South Carolina corn tastes especially delicious when it is prepared this way. You can make roasted corn the same way as the Catawba.*

Here's What You Need

Servings: 2
Recipe requires adult help.

Ingredients
- [ ] 2 ears of corn
- [ ] 2 tablespoons (30 ml) vegetable oil

Equipment
- [ ] small bowl
- [ ] vegetable brush
- [ ] large bowl
- [ ] grill (charcoal or gas)
- [ ] metal tongs with long handles

*Recipe from the written text of the Catawba people. Used with permission.

Here's What You Do

1 Gently pull back the husks of the corn, but do not remove them. Remove the silks.

2 Put the oil in the small bowl. Use the brush to coat the corn with the oil. Pull the husks back over the corn. Remove one strip of husk and use it to tie the rest of the husks closed around the open end of the cob.

3 Soak the corn in a large bowl of water for about 1 hour.

4 *Ask an adult* to light the grill. When the grill is hot, *ask an adult* to place the corn on the grill, using the tongs, and roast for about 10 to 15 minutes, turning the corn occasionally, until the husks turn brown. *Ask an adult* to use the tongs to remove the corn from the grill. When the corn has cooled, remove the husks and share this delicious food with a friend.

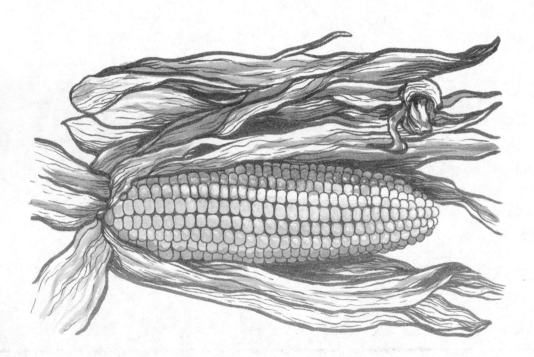

When we have our major festival, Yap Ye Iswa [yahb yang EES-wong], which is held the Saturday after Thanksgiving, we soak the ears overnight without removing the silks or placing oil on the corn. The ears are thrown directly into a fire pit and roasted until the husks turn brown. This is the best way to be able to serve thousands of people that come through the festival. Our guests stand in line for their turn to devour an ear!

DR. WENONAH HAIRE, CATAWBA

Cherokee Word Book

My Cherokee Word Book

The Cherokee (CHAIR-uh-kee) originally lived in what is now western North Carolina, the South Carolina foothills of the present-day Appalachian Mountains, Tennessee, eastern Kentucky, Alabama, Georgia, West Virginia, and southwest Virginia. They lived in villages that were surrounded by walls made from tall, thick tree trunks tied together. **Saplings** (small trees) were woven between the trunks, and finally the entire structure was covered with clay or mud. The roof was made with woven saplings that were covered with pieces of bark or thatch. This home-building method using woven saplings covered with mud was called **wattle and daub.** The Cherokee grew corn, beans, squash, sunflowers, melons, and other foods outside the walls of the village, and hunting parties went out to get game, such as bear, deer, and rabbit, for the entire village. They crafted baskets using the inner bark of the elm, oak, and cane, and made basket dyes from nuts (black walnut for a brownish color), fruits (elderberries for a rose color), and other natural materials.

After the Europeans arrived in the 1500s, it was only a matter of time before the Cherokee began losing their homelands. Cotton farmers wanted more land, and the discovery of gold in 1829 brought more immigrants. In 1830, the U.S. Congress passed the Indian Removal Act, forcing native peoples from their lands. Today the Cherokee Nation is the second largest nation in the United States (the Navajo are the largest), and almost half of the 200,000 tribal citizens live within the jurisdictional area of the Cherokee Nation, which is a 14-county area in northeastern Oklahoma. The Eastern band of Cherokee live on trust lands in western North Carolina. Other bands of Cherokee live throughout the United States, including the Echota Cherokee tribe of Alabama, the United Keetoowah bands of Cherokee in Oklahoma, and bands in Virginia, Kentucky, Georgia, Arkansas, and Texas. The name Cherokee is from the word Achere-akeon, which means "Fire Keepers." The Cherokee's original name, Keetoowah (KEE-too-wah), means "Those of the Chosen Town."

CHEROKEE FIGHT FOR SURVIVAL

The Cherokee fought relocation, and in 1832 the Supreme Court ruled in their favor. President Andrew Jackson ignored this ruling and began the removal process. In the winter of 1838–39, fourteen thousand Cherokee were forced to walk almost 1,000 miles (1,600 km) through five states to reach Indian Territory, present-day Oklahoma. About 4,000 people died on this journey, which has become known as the Trail of Tears. Countless others died prior to the Trail while in internment camps and after arrival in Indian Territory due to the effects of the journey.

CHEROKEE TRADITION

Gatiyo (gah-TEE-oh), or the stomp dance, is a traditional spiritual ceremony of the Southeastern nations. For the Cherokee, it is a time for the people to gather, enjoy a feast, play stickball, and dance all night. The leader, or chief, begins the chanting song and starts to dance in a winding line around a sacred fire that was built at early dawn by a designated fire starter. Dancers join in. Men and boys sing while women and girls provide rhythm by rattling **shackles** (something that confines the legs or arms) worn around each leg. Traditionally, the shackles are made from turtle shells filled with small stones, then tied together. As many as 12 shackles can be worn on each leg. During the dance, women stamp their feet, creating a rhythm with the chanters. The stomp dance can last well into the night.

Sequoyah was a Cherokee scholar who invented a way of coding the language of his people. He had watched white people reading newspapers and books and called this method of communication "talking leaves." Using some letters of the English alphabet as a guideline, Sequoyah created a Cherokee syllabary consisting of 84 characters, which make up the Cherokee language. It took him 12 years to create this system, which he completed in 1821. Sequoyah had done such a good job that a short time later, most Cherokee could read their language. This led to the first native publication, the *Cherokee Phoenix*. California's giant *Sequoia* redwood trees are named after Sequoyah. To honor Sequoyah's contribution, you can learn to say and write a traditional and a contemporary Cherokee greeting.

Here's What You Need

- [ ] 7 sheets of construction paper in a variety of colors, 8¹/₂ by 11 inches (21.5 by 28 cm) each
- [ ] markers in a variety of colors
- [ ] three-hole punch
- [ ] scissors
- [ ] 36 inches (93 cm) of yarn or string
- [ ] ruler

Here's What You Do

1. Use one sheet of construction paper for each greeting, phrase, or reply. Turn the paper so that the long edge is at the top. With a marker, write the heading at the top of the paper. Under the heading, write the Cherokee word. Write the pronunciation for the word under it, and write the meaning of the word under the pronunciation. Vary the marker colors as you like. Copy all the words on the list shown here. (The words and pronunciations listed here are from the Echota Cherokee tribe of Alabama. Spellings and pronunciations among the various Cherokee groups may vary.)

Traditional Cherokee Greeting
Aseyu (ah-say-YOU).
It is good (to see you).

Contemporary Greeting
Siyo (see-YOH).
Hello.

Greeting Phrase
Siyo, gado hadane, kohi iga (see-YOH, gah-DOH hah-dah-NAY, koh-HEE EE-gah).
Hello, what's happening (this day or) today?

Reply to Phrase
Osd (oh-oh-STAH).
Real good.

Final Reply
Nahinei (ha-hee-NAY)?
And you?

2 After you have written all of the words, use the punch to make three holes in each sheet of paper. Use the two remaining sheets for the front and back covers and punch holes in these sheets. Give your book a title and write it on the front cover. You might call it "My Cherokee Word Book" or whatever you like.

3 Assemble your book in this order: traditional greeting, contemporary greeting, greeting phrase, reply to phrase, and final reply. Put the two covers in place. Cut three pieces of yarn, each about 12 inches (31 cm) long.

4 Slip a piece of yarn through each of the three holes and tie the ends in a bow.

5 After you put the book together, memorize the greetings and use them with your friends. Don't forget to teach your friends so they can use the greetings, too.

My Cherokee Word Book

Contemporary Greeting
Siyo (see-YOH).
Hello.

> " *I remember watching my grandmother make soap,
> watching my grandfather use white oak to make our
> chairs.... They taught us our language, to respect
> nature, and how to use plants and animals for
> medicinal purposes. They taught us how to behave.* "
>
> JENNIE MAE TERRAPIN, CHEROKEE

THE TRADITION CONTINUES

HENRY WASHBURN, EUCHEE ELDER

Henry Washburn, or k' asA (kuh AH-say), as he is known in his native language, is an elder in the Euchee (YU-chee) tribe. He is one of about ten Euchee left who can speak the Euchee language fluently, and he feels strongly about teaching the language to children and adults in his community. Henry, along with other elders in the community, started a language class about 15 years ago. Children and adults gather throughout the year at the Picket Chapel United Methodist Church outside Sapulpa, Oklahoma, and at various locations in Sapulpa, where they learn words and phrases by playing Euchee *Jeopardy!* and Euchee bingo. The main goal of the Euchee elders is to pass on the spoken language to people in the community, since their language has always been one of oral, not written, tradition. Here are two Euchee words you can learn: *grandmother* is *gO laha* (GO lah-ha), and *grandfather* is *gO chO-O* (GO chuh-OH).

> *The sun is the most important natural symbol of how God arranged life. It continues its cycle, rising, [then] it sets (dies) and returns in the east, as man's soul does.*
>
> HENRY WASHBURN, EUCHEE ELDER

III
THE PLAINS

The Plains cover a large area of North America, from Canada to the Gulf of Mexico and from east of the the Rocky Mountains to west of the Mississippi River Valley. This region is divided into the northern, central, and southern Plains. The native peoples of the Plains all depended on the buffalo for survival. Southern Plains tribes, such as the Osage, established villages, constructed earth lodges, and farmed the land. Men went in hunting parties to hunt the buffalo and returned to the village after the hunt. The Gros Ventre, a northern Plains tribe, and the Lakota, a central Plains tribe, moved their camps to follow the buffalo. Most of these tribes lived in tepees, which were easier to take apart, move to a new location, and reassemble. Lakota women constructed the tepee while the men painted on the designs, which differed from tribe to tribe and always had meaning. With two layers of skin, the tepee provided insulation in winter. The tepee was considered a sacred place, the floor representing Mother Earth, the covering representing Father Sky, and the poles linking the people with the heavens. Some Plains nations today include the Blackfoot, Crow, Cheyenne, Ponca, Arapaho, Comanche, Kiowa, and Hidatsa.

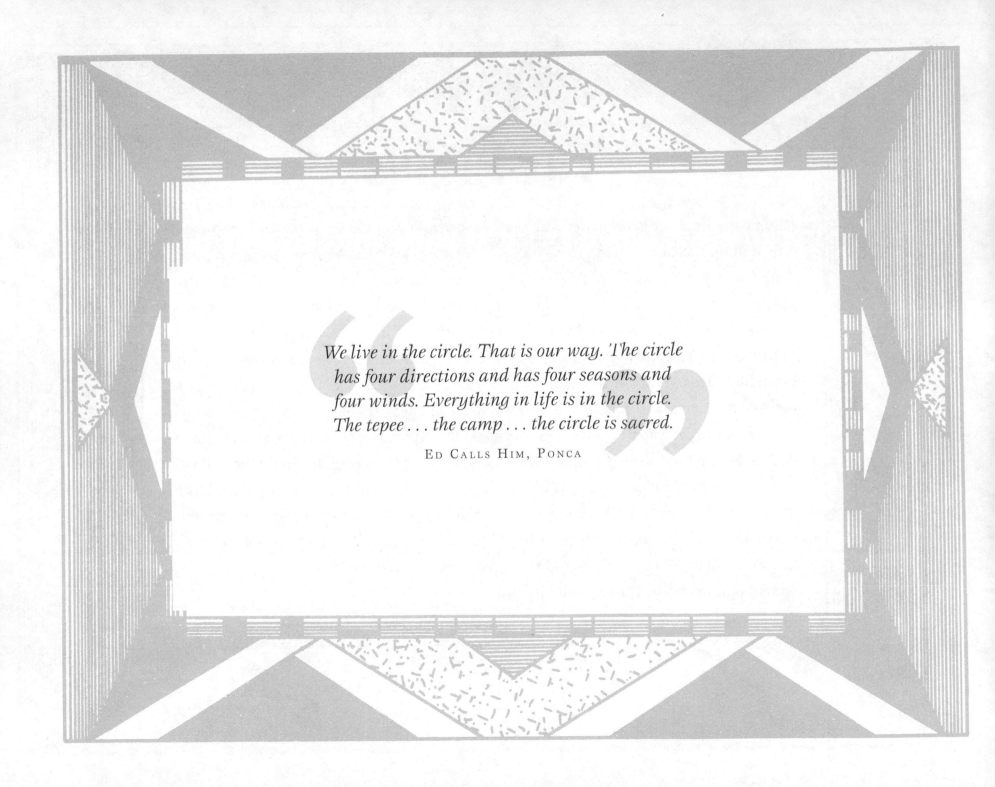

We live in the circle. That is our way. The circle has four directions and has four seasons and four winds. Everything in life is in the circle. The tepee . . . the camp . . . the circle is sacred.

Ed Calls Him, Ponca

Osage Finger-Weaving Belt

The Osage originally lived in an area that is now western Missouri, and in parts of Kansas, Oklahoma, and Arkansas. A southern Plains tribe, they set up villages along the Missouri and Osage Rivers, lived in earth lodges, and raised corn, beans, and squash. The men hunted buffalo twice a year in large communal hunting parties. The Osage followed a clan society, which was inherited through the father, and many continuc this tradition today. Symbolically, all the names of the clans and clan subdivisions represent all the forces of the universe. The two main clans are the Sky People, or Tsi-zhu (ZEE-jew), and the Earth People, or Ho'-E-Ga (HUNG-ghi), the warriors.

OSAGE HELP DEFEND AMERICA

When the U.S. Congress declared war on Japan in 1941, Osage war drums sounded, calling members of the tribe to fight the enemy. Major General Clarence L. Tinker, an Osage, became the first Native American to achieve a general's rank since the Civil War, when Stand Watie, Cherokee, became brigadier general.

We grew up as a close-knit family. . . . My grandparents would gather the family in the summer at my aunt's house to dry corn that was cut from the cob. It would be laid out in the sun to dry and would take several days to [dry]. All the younger children always enjoyed this time to get together.

JANET GOODFOX, OSAGE

As more white settlers moved into Osage territory, their lands began to diminish. In 1825, the Osage agreed to give up their land in Missouri and Arkansas to other tribes who were being pushed out of their territories. In 1870, the U.S. Congress passed an act that required the Osage to sell their land in Kansas. From that sale, they purchased 1.5 million acres (404,686 ha) of land in Oklahoma. Then, in the early 1900s, the Osage negotiated successfully with the U.S. government to retain all mineral rights under the surface of their land in Osage County, Oklahoma. With the discovery of oil on their land, the Osage Nation became wealthy. Today the nation continues to manage these resources for its economic growth. Many Osage live on this land in and around Pawhuska, Hominy, and Fairfax (Grayhorse), the three Osage districts in Oklahoma, or in cities in the United States and abroad. The Osage call themselves Wazhazhe (wah-SHAH-she).

Finger weaving, or flat braiding, is an old art of weaving thread or yarn without a loom. It is called finger weaving because the fingers pick up and hold certain threads during the weaving process. The Osage created beautiful designs, such as the chevron, the arrow and the diagonal weave, for pouches and headbands; streamers worn from the waist at the side of the body in men's ceremonial dress; men's garters worn at the knees with bells wrapped around the knees over the garters; and women's belts worn over skirts. Finger weaving continues as a traditional art form. In this project, you will make a belt using traditional Osage finger-weaving techniques.

OSAGE TRADITION

Traditional Osage ceremonial dances, called *i'n-lon-schka* (EE-lah-sh-kah), are held every June on three different weekends in the three Osage districts of Pawhuska, Hominy, and Fairfax (Grayhorse), Oklahoma. The dances are very structured and dancers must follow the rules. When a man or boy wants to participate, he must prepare his clothes and enter the dance a special way. Upon the dancer's entering the dance with his family, the head committeeman places the **roach** (headdress) and the eagle feather on the dancer, and then he is given a place among the other dancers. Some of the other participants include drum keepers, tail dancers, whip men, and women singers.

Here's What You Need

- [ ] tape measure
- [ ] scissors
- [ ] 2 skeins of wool yarn* in blue and yellow
- [ ] ruler
- [ ] pencil or wooden dowel the size of a pencil
- [ ] masking tape
- [ ] paperweight

*Wool yarn is strong, holds its shape well, and lasts long. If you are allergic to wool, you can use cotton or acrylic yarn.

Here's What You Do

1 Use the tape measure to measure around your waist. Remember the number.

2 Cut six blue strands and six yellow strands of yarn, each measuring 60 inches (152 cm) long.

3 Lay the strands out on your work surface, alternating colors, starting with blue on the left. Lay the pencil across the strands about 4 inches (10 cm) from the bottom. Tape both ends of the pencil to your work surface.

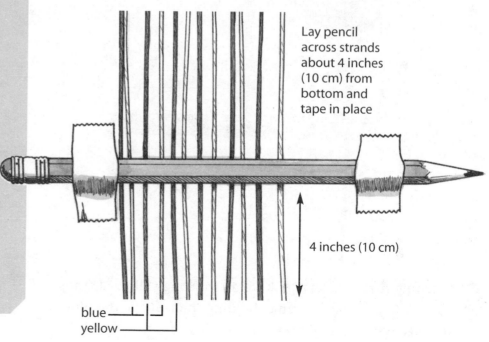

Lay pencil across strands about 4 inches (10 cm) from bottom and tape in place

4 inches (10 cm)

blue
yellow

4 Starting with the first blue strand at the left, loop the top, long end of the strand over the pencil so that it is now pointing down, and loop the bottom, short end over the pencil so that it is pointing up. Use the paperweight to hold the short end in place.

5 Repeat step 4 with the other strands until they all are looped around the pencil. Remove the paperweight and tape the short ends of the strands to your work surface.

Loop short end of first blue strand up and anchor with paperweight

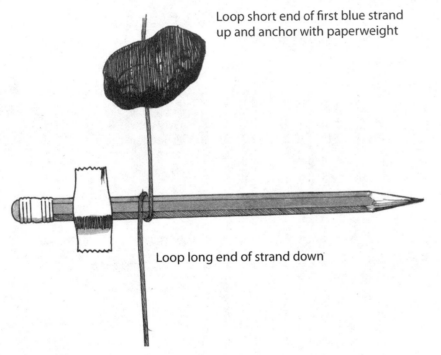

Loop long end of strand down

6 Working from the left, pick up all the long yellow strands in your hand, one at a time, holding them above the blue strands, which are flat on your work surface.

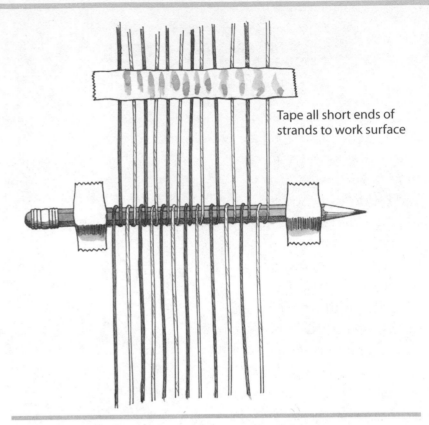

Tape all short ends of strands to work surface

Art Tip It is important to make sure that the long yarn strands *never* crisscross as you start to weave. The blue and yellow strands must always alternate.

7 Take the first long blue strand on the left and lay it across the other blue strands, placing it close to the pencil as shown. Lay the yellow strands down, placing them in between the blue strands.

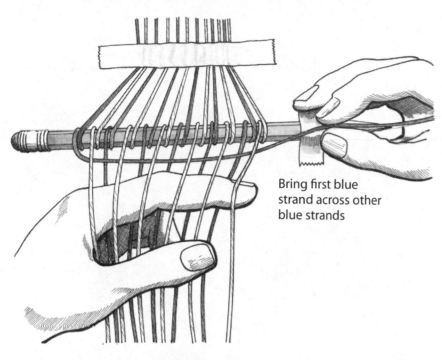

Bring first blue strand across other blue strands

Pick up all yellow strands

As you weave, pull the strands that are held in your hand as well as the ones that go across so that you have a tight weave, but don't pull too tightly.

9 Repeat steps 6 to 8 until you've woven about eight rows.

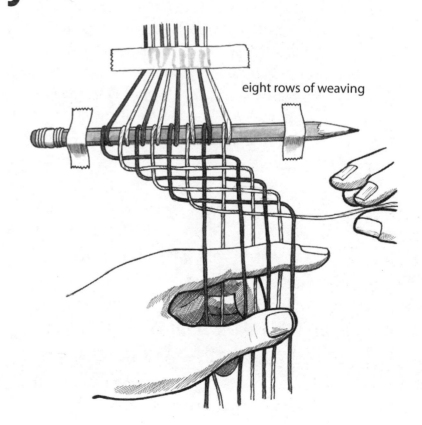

eight rows of weaving

8 Working from the left again, pick up all the blue strands, one at a time, holding them above the yellow strands, which are flat on your work surface. Take the first yellow strand on the left and lay it across the other yellow strands, placing it close to the blue strand near the pencil. Lay the blue strands down, placing them in between the yellow strands.

10 Continue weaving until the belt measures about 12 to 16 inches (31 to 41 cm) longer than your waist measurement. As you weave, you'll notice the strands will get closer together. It's important to continue to keep the strand colors alternating—never crossing one over the other.

11 Cut two pieces of yarn, each about 12 inches (30.5 cm) long. Set one aside. Wrap the other strand around the end of the weaving and tie it in a tight knot. Cut the fringe to about 2 inches (5 cm). Untape the pencil and gently pull it through the yarn loops. Tie the other 12-inch (30.5-cm) strand around the end of the weaving in a tight knot. Cut the fringe on this end to about 2 inches (5 cm), and you're done. Wear the belt with your jeans or a skirt and tie it loosely, letting the ends hang down.

We taught our children to get ready to dance . . . when they were very young . . . and now our grandchildren are learning. [We are] keeping our tradition, keeping our culture, keeping our dancing. I think that's real important. We help our children, we help their children, to keep their culture.

AMOS GOODFOX, OSAGE AND PAWNEE

Lakota Beaded Wristband

In the early 1800s, the Lakota (lah-KOH-tah), Dakota, and Nakota dominated the Plains, which included what is now North and South Dakota, northern Nebraska, eastern Wyoming, and southeastern Montana. The buffalo was important to their existence and way of life. They moved about the Plains to follow this important animal. The buffalo provided food, clothing, shelter, and tools. The hide tepee was a logical choice for a dwelling because it could be moved more easily than other types of dwellings. When the United States purchased the Louisiana Territory from the French in 1803, white settlers made their way westward onto Lakota lands. By the mid-1800s, the buffalo were almost exterminated, seriously threatening the survival of the Lakota and other Plains tribes. The Lakota and other Plains tribes were given reservation lands in 1868 that included most of present-day South Dakota and the Black Hills.

IN THE LAKOTA LANDS

When Colonel George Custer discovered gold in the Black Hills in 1874, **prospectors** (people who explore an area for mineral deposits) swarmed the area. The lands belonged to the Lakota and other tribes. To protect the home of the Great Spirit, Wakan Tanka, in the Black Hills in South Dakota, from being mined for gold, the great Oglala warrior Chief Crazy Horse and the Hunkpapa Chief Sitting Bull led a resistance against Custer, defeating his troops in the Battle of the Little Bighorn.

The Lakota include seven bands: the Hunkpapa, Miniconjou, Oglala, Sicanju, Itazipco, Oohenunpa, and Sihasapa. In 1889, the U.S. Congress divided the Sioux reservation into six smaller reservations in North and South Dakota, where many Lakota and other tribes live today. Their own name, Lakota, means "Common People" or "Allies."

Lakota women decorated items such as clothes, robes, and cradleboards with designs in **quillwork** (ornamentation of a hide for decorative purposes by applying porcupine quills in a variety of ways). When the Europeans introduced glass beads to the Lakota, the women used beads in their designs, though quillwork never died out. The Lakota are well known for their beautiful bead- and quillwork designs. The southern Plains tribes, such as the Kiowa, create intricate, delicate designs. The northern Plains tribes, such as the Lakota, produce bolder, more striking designs. You will make a Lakota beaded wristband that is based on a very old design, the mountain design. (You can finish your wristband in a week if you do a little bit each day.)

> "*Many people view us as superhuman or subhuman. We're not that way. We're just logical humans. For instance, logically, if you do bad things, then of course bad things happen. If you do good things in your life, good things happen. Everything you do in your life, good or bad, affects everyone else.*"
>
> BARBARA FREE SPIRIT SHUPE, OGLALA LAKOTA

LAKOTA TRADITION

The Lakota have a saying, *mitakuye oyasin* (mee-TOCK-ku-yay OY-yay-sheen), which means "we are all related." They believe that everything serves an important purpose in this life—the trees, the animals, the plants, the earth, and the people. The Lakota have a deep respect for all things in nature and live by the four Lakota values: bravery, wisdom, generosity, and respect.

Here's What You Need

- ruler
- pen
- 9-by-5-inch (23-by-13-cm) piece of denim fabric (cut from old jeans)
- seed beads (white, blue, green, and red, orange, or yellow)*
- 4 plastic single-serving applesauce cups, clean and empty, or shallow bowls
- beading thread*
- beading needle*
- scissors
- self-adhesive Velcro
- fabric glue

*You can find seed beads, beading thread, and beading needles at any craft or discount store, such as Kmart or Wal-Mart.

Here's What You Do

1 Using the ruler and pen, draw a 5-by-2$\frac{1}{2}$-inch (13-by-6-cm) rectangle in the center of the piece of denim. Draw three lines across the rectangle about $\frac{5}{8}$ inch (1.5 cm) apart, spaced evenly along the 2$\frac{1}{2}$-inch (6-cm) side.

Draw a 5-by-2$\frac{1}{2}$-inch (13-by-6-cm) rectangle on the denim

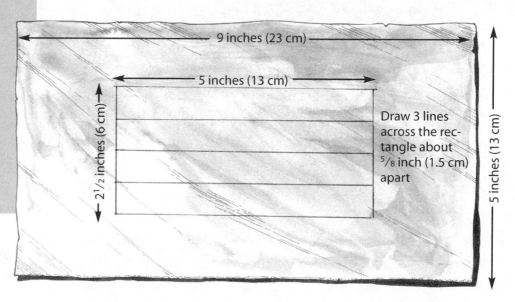

2 Look at the pattern shown for the mountain design before you start beading so that you understand the placement of the colors. Each color block will always have eight rows and eight beads to a row.

Each color block has 8 rows and 8 beads to a row

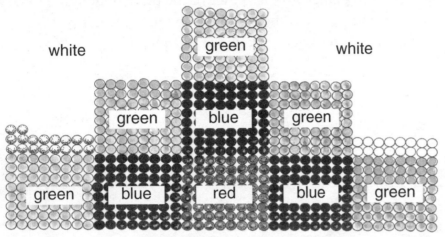

white   green   white

green   blue   green

green   blue   red   blue   green

For mountains, use blue and green

For central fire, use red, yellow, or orange

Entire beaded area around mountain design is white

3 Put the beads in the applesauce cups, one color per cup. Set these aside.

4 Thread the beading needle using a single thickness of thread and knot the end of the thread. Gently push the needle up through the back of the denim, coming out the front of the denim at the lower right corner of the rectangle. You will make the first row of beads between the bottom of the rectangle and the line above.

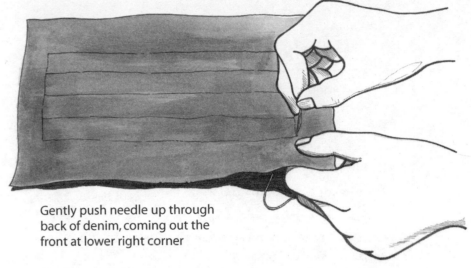

Gently push needle up through back of denim, coming out the front at lower right corner

Art Tip An easy way to get the tiny beads on the needle is to slide or drag the needle through the beads in the cup. You should be able to pick up anywhere from two to four beads at a time. Keep doing this until you have threaded eight beads altogether.

5 Thread eight white beads on the needle and let them slide all the way to the end of the thread close to the fabric. Take the needle up to the line above and make a small stitch from right to left, gently pushing the needle in and out through the front of the fabric as shown. The beads should form a straight, vertical line.

7 Continue beading, following the mountain design and changing colors as necessary. When your thread runs out, push it through the front of the fabric and out the back. Stitch over this stitch three times, then cut the thread on the back of the fabric. Thread the needle again, knot the end of the thread, and push the needle up through the back of the fabric where you just ended and out the front. Continue beading the rest of the bottom row. When you get to the end (left side) of the bottom row, bead the next row up, working from left to right. Continue beading the other rows as shown.

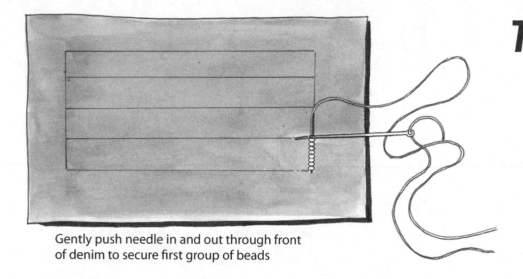

Gently push needle in and out through front of denim to secure first group of beads

6 Thread eight white beads on the needle, let them slide down to the end of the thread close to the fabric, then make a small stitch on the end line just to the left of where you began beading.

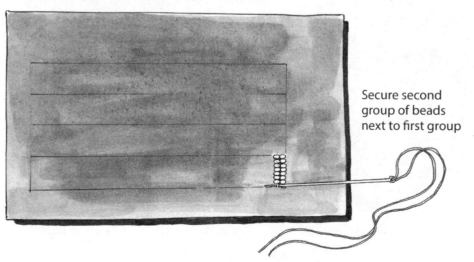

Secure second group of beads next to first group

Bead other rows same as first row

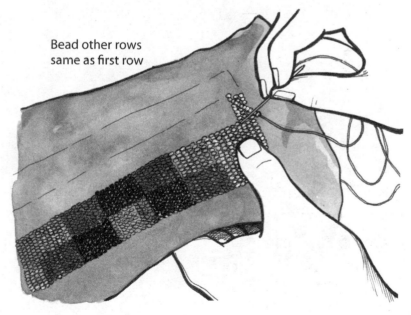

8 When all the rows are beaded, cut along the two long edges of the design to get rid of the extra denim, making sure to leave a ¼-inch (.5-cm) border.

9 Wrap the wristband around your wrist until it fits comfortably. Attach the Velcro to the two short edges to close your wristband. Place the softer piece of Velcro on the right side (front) of the right short edge. Place the rougher piece of Velcro on the wrong side (back) of the left short edge.

10 Cut off any excess denim from the two short edges, cutting close to the Velcro. Squeeze a thin layer of fabric glue around the entire edge of the wristband. This will keep the edges from fraying. Let it dry completely.

"I was born and raised on the reservation. When I was a child, I remember going to powwows with my family. These were gatherings of the people. Many people dressed in regalia and danced to the sound of the drums. We ate good food and got to visit with other relatives and friends. It was a fun time for us.

CANDACE LEE ELKNATION,
MINICONJOU LAKOTA

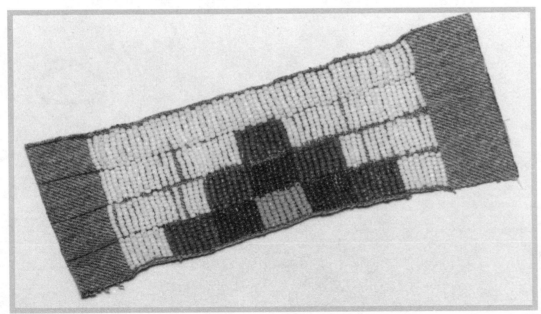

THE TRADITION CONTINUES

JANET GOODFOX, OSAGE RIBBON-WORK ARTIST

Janet Goodfox, Osage, lives and works in the Washington, D.C., area. She finds time in her busy schedule to continue a traditional art form called ribbon work. She learned by watching her grandmother and with the help of a friend. Ribbon work is the principal design element used on ceremonial clothes worn for traditional Osage ceremonial dances, called *i'n-lon-schka*. The geometric patterns and colors used are associated with the wearer's clan. Ribbon work involves layering about eight strips of different colored ribbons, one on top of the other. Starting on the bottom row, marks are made with a pencil to measure cut marks on the design. The design is clipped with scissors along the cut marks, and then the clipped fabric is turned under like a hem and sewn down with tiny stitches. Repeating the clipping and sewing brings different colors to the surface of the design.

> *These are patterns from my grandmother that she made. . . . She was smart enough to save these little pieces. . . . I use all of my grandmother's patterns. I like old patterns.*
>
> JANET GOODFOX, OSAGE RIBBON-WORK ARTIST

49

IV

THE SOUTHWEST

The Southwest includes parts of the southwestern United States and areas of north-western Mexico. Although the land is beautiful, with rugged canyons, pine-covered mountains, flat mesas, and cactus-filled deserts set against a bright blue sky, to an outsider the environment can be harsh, with hot summer days, cold nights, and scarce rainfall. But the Native Americans of the Southwest never saw it that way. They successfully grew crops in the arid soil and gathered wild plants and roots. Prehistoric inhabitants, such as the Anasazi, lived in cliff dwellings toward the end of their existence. Descendants of these cliff dwellers occupied a large part of this region and were named the Pueblo people by their Spanish-speaking neighbors. *Pueblo* is a Spanish word meaning "town." The name probably derives from the adobe communities they built. **Adobe** is sun-dried brick made of clay and straw. The Pueblo's more nomadic neighbors, the Apache, relied on hunting and gathering to make a living. Some Southwestern nations today include Mohave, Navajo, Zuni, Acoma, Hopi, Tewa, Jemez, and Laguna.

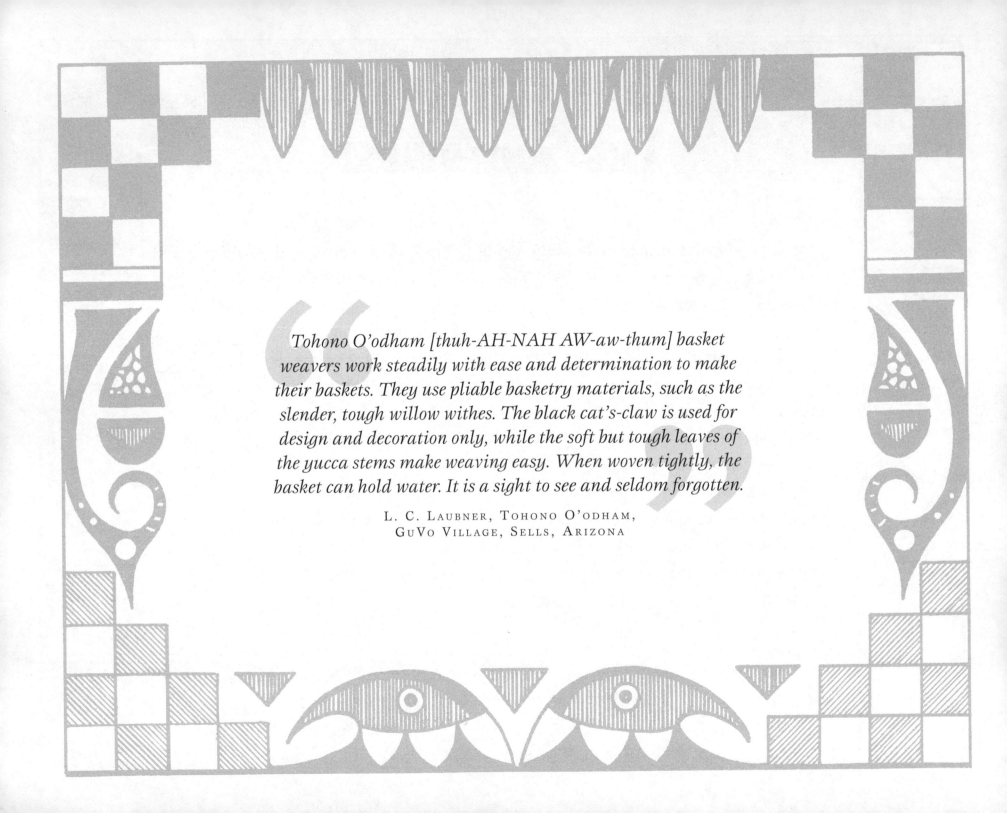

> *Tohono O'odham [thuh-AH-NAH AW-aw-thum] basket weavers work steadily with ease and determination to make their baskets. They use pliable basketry materials, such as the slender, tough willow withes. The black cat's-claw is used for design and decoration only, while the soft but tough leaves of the yucca stems make weaving easy. When woven tightly, the basket can hold water. It is a sight to see and seldom forgotten.*

L. C. LAUBNER, TOHONO O'ODHAM,
GUVO VILLAGE, SELLS, ARIZONA

Navajo Woven Wall Hanging

The Navajo (NAH-vuh-ho) have lived in what is now New Mexico, Arizona, and Utah for many years, having migrated to the area from the subarctic more than 900 years ago. Many elders today remember life as it was when they were young. They had to milk goats daily; tend the sheep, which were introduced to the Navajo by the Spaniards in the fifteenth century, and prepare the wool for weaving; plant, harvest, dry, and grind corn on grinding stones to make flour for tortillas; gather wild potatoes, and hunt rabbits and prairie dogs for food. There were no indoor ovens in their traditional dwellings, the hogans (HO-gons). The Navajo wove beautiful rugs from sheep's wool, crafted baskets used as storage containers, and made exquisite silver and turquoise jewelry. Many Navajo continue these traditional ways but have adopted modern ways, such as having a more formalized government with elected officials.

NAVAJO DWELLING

Hogans are built according to instructions that were given to the people by the First Man and First Woman in the Navajo creation story. The entrance always faces east to greet the morning sun of Father Sky. The inside of the hogan represents Mother Earth's womb. And the mud, rock, and wood of which the hogan is made surround the Navajo in a protective way. Wood posts made of juniper are placed upright in the ground in a circle to form the frame. Additional logs are placed in between the posts. The roof is also made with logs, and any remaining spaces or small openings are filled in with mud, wood chips, and bark. Today many Navajo live in modern-style houses, but also have a hogan that is used for ceremonies.

With the arrival of Europeans in the area in the fourteenth and fifteenth centuries, Navajo lands were threatened. Although treaties to protect their land were established between the Navajo and the United States, like most other treaties they were not honored and the U.S. Army forced the Navajo to move. They refused to leave and many hid in Navajo Mountain and Canyon de Chelly. But in 1864, Christopher Houston "Kit" Carson forced 8,000 Navajo to walk 300 miles (483 km) to Fort Sumner, New Mexico, which became known as the Long Walk during which almost 200

Navajo died. They stayed in confinement in Fort Sumner for four years and finally were returned to their land, where they continue to live on the largest reservation in the United States. They call themselves Diné (din-EH), which means "the People."

SELF-GOVERNMENT

With the passage of the Indian Reorganization Act in 1934, the U.S. government recognized tribal governments as sovereign nations. Each nation organizes its government differently. The Navajo have an elected council and president. Each town or village has a "chapter" of members elected by the community. The chapter takes care of local business. In 1975, the Cheyenne and Arapaho tribes of Oklahoma adopted their current constitution, which established a business committee of four elected Cheyenne members and four elected Arapaho members.

NAVAJO TRADITION

The Navajo believe that it is very important to walk in the beautyway throughout life. Walking in the beautyway means that you are walking in balance and inner harmony with yourself and with all things around you.

For centuries, Navajo weavers have used upright **looms** (frames for interlacing two or more threads or yarns to make cloth) of their own design to produce wool blankets and rugs with complex designs and patterns. Each design has a name, usually from the region in which the rug was first made. Some examples include Chinle, Ganado, Crystal, and Two Grey Hills. The Chief blanket design was named to honor the chiefs from other tribes with whom the Navajo traded. Women who continue traditional weaving raise their own sheep; shear, wash, card, and spin the wool; and dye the wool using natural plants, such as lichen, rabbit brush, and wild walnut. The entire process may take as long as one to two months. Some rugs are woven so tightly, they are practically waterproof. In this activity, you can weave a small, simple Navajo wall hanging using some elements of the Chinle design.

Here's What You Need

- pencil
- ruler
- piece of heavy cardboard
- sharp scissors
- small skein of cotton yarn in cream or white
- 4 skeins of wool yarn in black, dark (not bright) red, white, and gray
- yarn needle
- clean hair comb

Here's What You Do

1 Draw a 7-by-5¾-inch (18-by-14.5-cm) rectangle on the heavy cardboard and cut it out. Along each short edge of the rectangle, cut 22 notches ¼ inch (.5 cm) apart. Cut each notch about ¼ inch (.5 cm) deep. This will be your loom.

2 Cut a piece of cotton yarn about 8 yards (7 m) long. This is the **warp** (stationary strands on a loom). Start the warp on your loom by putting it through the bottom left notch, leaving an 8-inch (20-cm) tail out the back of the loom. Wrap the yarn around the loom, working from bottom to top and left to right through each notch in turn. When you reach the top right notch, leave an 8-inch (20-cm) tail out the back of the loom. Turn the loom over, back faceup, and tie the two tails together in a tight knot.

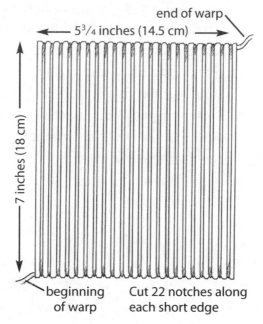

end of warp
5¾ inches (14.5 cm)
7 inches (18 cm)
beginning of warp
Cut 22 notches along each short edge

3 Cut a piece of red yarn about 84 inches (213 cm) long and thread it on the needle. This will be the **weft** (strands that are woven into the warp).

4 Start to weave right to left at the bottom right corner of the loom. Begin by placing the needle *under* the first warp, *over* the second, *under* the third, and so on until you reach the left end of the loom. Gently pull the weft all the way through, leaving a 4-inch (10-cm) tail on the right. For the second row, weave back toward the right side of the loom, placing the needle *under* the first left warp, *over* the second, and so on until you reach the right side. Pull the weft gently, making sure the warp on the left and right ends doesn't "pull in." Use the comb to **pack** (push down) each row very close to the previous one. *Do this each time you weave a new row.*

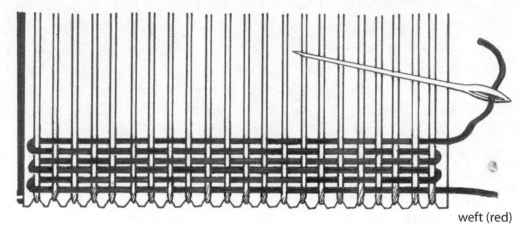

weft (red)

Weave under and over across each row, packing rows close together

Art Tip

When a color runs out or you change colors, start the same or new color on either the right or left side of the loom. Remember to weave the new row opposite to the way you wove the previous row. Do not cut the yarn ends that are sticking out. You can do this when you're finished. Make sure yarn ends are about 2 inches (5 cm) long.

5 Continue weaving with the red yarn until it measures about ⅝ inch (1.5 cm). Now weave with the other colors following this pattern:

gray	¼ inch (.3 cm)		gray	¼ inch (.3 cm)
black	⅛ inch (.5 cm)		white	⅛ inch (.5 cm)
white	¼ inch (.3 cm)		black	⅝ inch (1.5 cm)
black	⅛ inch (.5 cm)		red	½ inch (1 cm)
gray	¼ inch (.3 cm)		gray	¼ inch (.3 cm)
red	½ inch (1 cm)		black	⅛ inch (.5 cm)
black	⅝ inch (1.5 cm)		white	¼ inch (.3 cm)
white	⅛ inch (.5 cm)		black	⅛ inch (.5 cm)
gray	¼ inch (.3 cm)		gray	¼ inch (.3 cm)
red	⅛ inch (.5 cm)		red	⅝ inch (1.5 cm)

6 The weaving should end at the top of the loom, all rows packed very tightly. If you followed the pattern and your weaving is not at the top of the loom, don't worry about it. It is time to end the weaving.

7 Turn the loom facedown and cut the unwoven warp across the middle, cutting through the two knotted strands, then turn the loom faceup again. Remove the warp strands from the notches along the bottom. Tie the first pair of strands on the left together in a knot close to the edge of the weaving. Tie the next pair of strands together, and so on until all pairs are tied. Repeat for the warp strands at the top of the weaving. Trim the warp strands to a length of about 1 inch (2.5 cm).

8 Carefully trim the yarn ends from the weft that are sticking out of the rows.

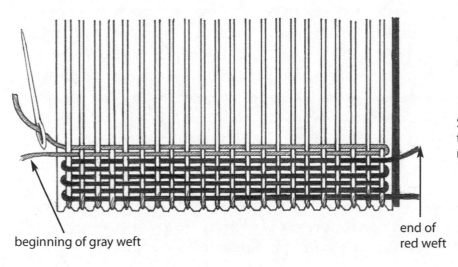

beginning of gray weft

end of red weft

Start a new color on either right or left side of loom, letting 2 inches (5 cm) of yarn ends stick out and weaving new row opposite to the way you wove previous row

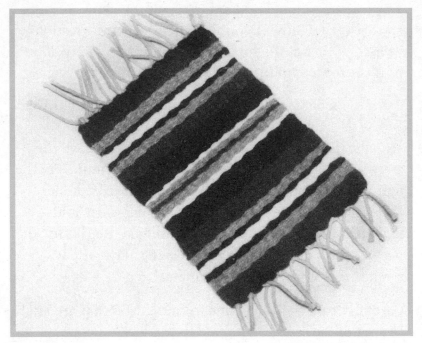

© Copyright 2000 Gary Braman

> *Corn is very important to the Navajo. It symbolizes the life cycle. We use corn pollen in our prayers.*
>
> LETTIE NAVE, NAVAJO

THE CODE TALKERS

During World War II (1939–45), the Navajo served in the Pacific in the U.S. Marines and transmitted messages by telephone and radio in their native language. The Japanese, who were noted for breaking military codes, were never able to break this code, since the Navajo language is very complex. The idea to use the Navajo for this mission came from Philip Johnston, the son of a Navajo missionary, who spoke the language because he was raised on the reservation. As a World War I veteran, he knew that the Choctaw language had been used to encode messages and believed the Navajo language could be used in the same way. In 1942, the first group of 29 Navajo recruits created a dictionary of military words and terms, which had to be memorized before they took their posts. They worked around the clock transmitting information on troop movements and military tactics, orders, and important communications. Eventually more than 400 Navajo served as code talkers. Major Howard Connor of the Fifth Marine Division commented that the Marines never would have been able to take Iwo Jima had it not been for the Navajo code talkers. In 1992, the Pentagon officially recognized the incredibly heroic efforts of these men, honoring 35 code talkers. Note: Many tribes served as code talkers in both World Wars. These included Cheyenne, Comanche, Cherokee, Choctaw, Osage, Sioux, Chippewa, Creek, Hopi, Kiowa, Menominee, Muscogee-Seminole, Oneida, Pawnee, and Sac & Fox.

Zuni Water Jar

The Zuni (ZOO-nee) have lived in what is now western New Mexico since long before Francisco Vásquez de Coronado, the Spanish explorer, arrived in Mexico in the sixteenth century. They may have migrated to the region from areas that are now part of Mexico and Arizona. The Zuni were not cliff dwellers like their other Pueblo neighbors. They constructed multistoried, apartment-type dwellings made of adobe, and grew corn, beans, and pumpkins. They used local natural resources, including clay from nearby mountains, to make pottery and silver for jewelry making.

When Coronado tried to force the Zuni to live by his country's rule, they resisted, but eventually they had to leave their original homeland, Hawikuh, to settle nearby in what is now their current pueblo. Today Zuni Pueblo is the most populous of the 17 pueblos in the Southwest, with about 12,000 residents. The Zuni call themselves A'Shiwi (AH-shih-wee), which means "People."

Today a large majority of Zuni craft jewelry for a living. Only a handful of Zuni are potters, but they are well known as expert potters. Traditionally, Zuni potters created items such as water jars that were carried on women's heads, bowls to carry cornmeal used during ceremonies, and dough bowls. Many continue to make pottery in these traditional styles and paint unique designs on each piece that are similar to the designs first painted by their ancestors. These designs and the shapes of the containers identify the pottery as typically Zuni.

ZUNI TRADITION

Before taking the clay from the mountain, Zuni potters, like Noreen Simplicio, say a prayer to Mother Earth asking her permission to take the clay so others can enjoy its beauty.

Traditional Zuni potters collect clay from nearby mountains; clean out the sand, rocks, and roots contained within; and prepare the clay. Next they shape the pot, sometimes using a coil method and often without the help of a potter's wheel. Then they air-dry the pot. After the pot is dry, the potters use sandpaper to smooth the surface, apply **slip** (a mixture of finely ground clay and water applied over the pot with a brush, cloth, or piece of leather to smooth and/or color it), let the piece dry again, polish it with a rubbing stone, paint on the design, and finally fire the pot in a **kiln** (oven, furnace, or

Here's What You Need

- [ ] small box of self-hardening or wet-set clay, about 5 pounds (2.27 kg)
- [ ] ruler
- [ ] craft paintbrush
- [ ] acrylic paints (white, brown, red, tan, and black)
- [ ] small bowl of water
- [ ] paper towel
- [ ] clear acrylic spray sealer (optional—requires adult help)

other heated enclosure used for processing an object by burning, firing, or drying). Your Zuni water jar will have a traditional shape and design.

Here's What You Do

1 Shape a piece of clay into a ball with a 2-inch (5-cm) diameter. Shape the ball into a shallow bowl and set it aside.

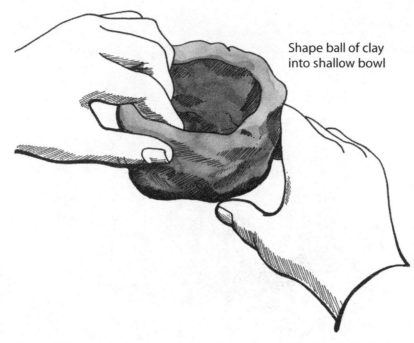

Shape ball of clay into shallow bowl

2 Use additional clay to make about six coils, each ¼ inch (.5 cm) thick. (You may use more coils depending on how you shape your bowl.) Make three of the coils about 10 to 12 inches (25 to 30 cm) long and the other three shorter, about 4 to 6 inches (10 to 15 cm). Place one of the long coils on the top edge of the bowl and gently blend or smooth it into the bowl with your fingers until you can no longer see where you attached it.

3 Place the other two long clay coils, one at a time, on the top edge of the bowl, continuing to smooth each coil into the bowl. This is the middle section of the bowl. Use your fingers to shape the middle section of the bowl as shown so that it is rounded.

4 Place the three shorter coils on the inside top edge, one at a time. If these coils are too long, break off any excess pieces of clay. Smooth and shape the jar so the opening starts to narrow. Let the jar dry completely.

Middle of bowl is rounded—use fingers to gently push out this section from inside

5 Paint the entire jar white unless you have used white clay, and let it dry. Paint on some traditional designs (see the illustrations on page 62), using the other colors. Remember to swish the paintbrush in the water and pat it dry on a paper towel before changing colors. Let the jar dry completely.

medallion

rain clouds

deer with heart line
(Breath of Life)

rainbird

6 Spray your jar with clear acrylic sealer if you want. *Do this outside with the help of an adult.* Let the jar dry completely. *Never put water or food in your jar. It is just for decoration.*

"As a child I always played with mud and made little mud pots and bowls. So I guess I always knew I would grow up to be a potter and be successful as an artist!"

Noreen Simplicio, Zuni

Tohono O'odham Basket

The Tohono O'odham have lived for more than 10,000 years in their original homeland in southern Arizona and northern Mexico, which is now called the Sonoran Desert. This environment may have been too difficult for others, but the Tohono O'odham adapted well, learning to harvest desert plants, such as mesquite beans for making flour and saguaro cactus fruit for making syrup and jam. They learned to use desert grasses and mud to construct homes. During the summer, they set up villages in the valleys and took advantage of summer rains to farm the dry soil. In the winter, they moved their villages to the mountains, where water was available from springs.

Because the Tohono O'odham's land was of little economic interest to explorers, contact with Europeans came late—not until the seventeenth century. When Spain took control of Mexico, the Tohono O'odham became subjects of the king, who let the Tohono O'odham retain title to their lands. But after Mexico gained its independence, the Tohono O'odham began losing land to the U.S. government due to mining and to settlers moving into their territory. In the early 1900s, the Tohono O'odham gained back some of their original land, where they continue to live today. Their name means "Desert People."

Today many Tohono O'odham continue their traditional ways, including basket weaving, and are considered excellent weavers. Traditional weavers gather all of their materials from the desert, including devil's-claw, white yucca, banana yucca, and bear grass. Weavers use traditional closed, wheat, and split stitches to produce baskets with unique designs. The well-known sacred design Man-in-the-Maze, a symbol of life, starts in the center of the basket and extends outward. In the design's center, the turns in the maze are numerous and are woven close together to signify the many turning points a person's life takes early on. As the design moves to the outer area of the basket, the turns in the maze lessen and are farther apart, signifying fewer turning points in later life. The basket you can make in this activity is made of yarn, but the weaving techniques you will use are similar to those of the master Tohono O'odham basket weavers.

Here's What You Do

1 Cut one strand of dark-colored yarn about 72 inches (183 cm) long and set it aside.

2 Take the light-colored skein of yarn and tape one end of the yarn to the left side of the back of a chair. Wrap the yarn around the back of the chair 20 times.

Here's What You Need

- scissors
- ruler
- 2 different skeins of dark-colored yarn (black, brown, or red)
- skein of white or tan yarn
- masking tape
- chair
- yarn needle

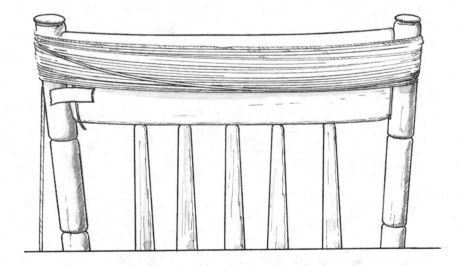

Wrap yarn around back of chair 20 times

3 Hold the wrapped strands close to the tape and cut through the strands. Continue to hold the strands as they fall away from the chair.

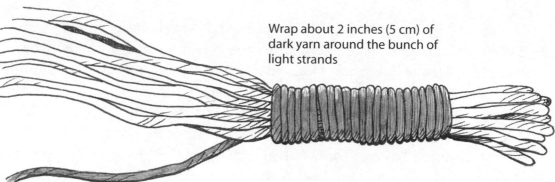

Wrap about 2 inches (5 cm) of dark yarn around the bunch of light strands

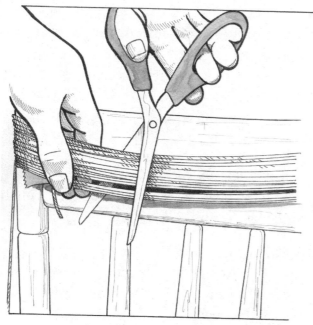

Hold wrapped yarn close to tape and cut through strands

5 Bend the wrapped end toward the bunch of light strands and hold the end in place. Wrap the dark yarn over the ends sticking out to secure them in place, then wrap the dark yarn around the light strands for another 1½ inches (4 cm).

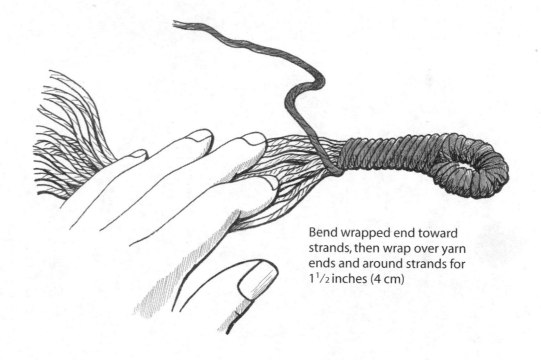

Bend wrapped end toward strands, then wrap over yarn ends and around strands for 1½ inches (4 cm)

4 Wrap the dark yarn strand you set aside around one end of the bunch of yarn strands you are holding. Keep wrapping in a spiral, keeping the dark yarn close together at each turn, until the dark yarn covers 2 inches (5 cm) of the bunch of light strands.

6 Thread the dark strand on the needle. Bend the wrapped end once more to make the beginnings of a coiled shape and hold the coil in place. Make your first stitch by pushing the needle down through the front edge of the coil and out the back. Bring the needle back to the front and make a second stitch next to the first one. This will anchor the coil to the strand bunch.

Bend wrapped end in a coil, then push needle down through front and out back of coil to anchor coil to strand bunch

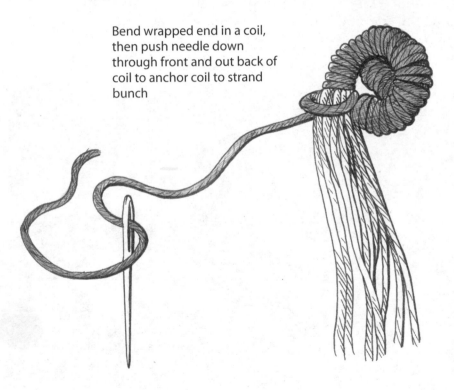

7 Continue to stitch, wrapping the strand bunch around the coil as you stitch so that the stitching anchors the strand bunch to the coil. When you run out of dark yarn, cut another strand, in either the same color or the other dark color, about 36 inches (91 cm) long. Thread this on the needle and make your first stitch by pushing the needle down through the front edge of the coil, out the back, and up around the strand bunch, leaving about a 2-inch (5-cm) tail of yarn. (Do not cut any tails that are sticking out. You can trim the loose ends when you are finished.) After each stitch, pull on the strand bunch so that the individual strands don't clump up.

8 Work in the wheat stitch, following these steps:

a. Start the stitch by pushing the needle down through the front edge of the coil and out the back.

b. Bring the needle around to the front and stick the needle through the original hole and out the back. Bring the needle around to the front and stick the needle through the original hole again. (You need to push the needle through three times when you begin a new stitch after you've run out of yarn. Otherwise, twice is enough.)

c. As you pull the yarn through, use your finger to move the dark yarn strands apart, forming a V. You can use the wheat stitch for your entire basket.

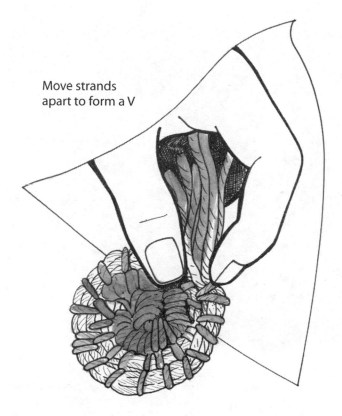

Move strands
apart to form a V

10 Up to this point, the stitched coil has been flat. To have the coiled rows begin to take the shape of a basket, place the strand bunch on top of the coiled row as you stitch. Build each new row on top of the previous row, using your fingers to shape the rows.

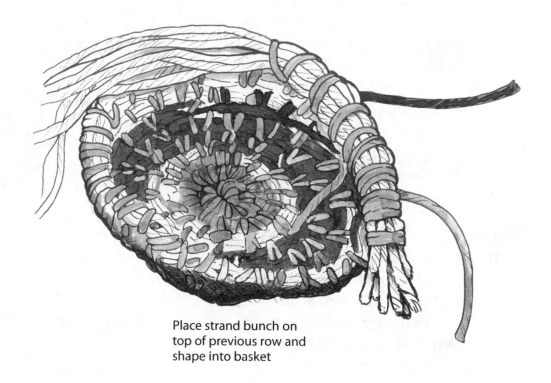

Place strand bunch on
top of previous row and
shape into basket

9 When you get to the end of the strand bunch, you will need to add more. Follow the directions in steps 2 and 3 to make a new strand bunch. However, this time wrap the yarn around the chair 30 times. Place the two bunches end to end, hold them in place, and continue stitching. There will be little ends of yarn sticking out where you joined the two bunches together. You can trim these later.

11 Continue weaving the basket until you have about 8 to 10 coiled rows. To finish the basket, stitch over the ends of the strand bunch until they are covered. To secure the yarn before you cut it, push the needle through a 2-inch (5-cm) section of a row, coming out the back of the basket, then cut the yarn. Trim any loose ends sticking out of your basket, and reshape the basket with your fingers if needed.

TOHONO O'ODHAM TRADITION

The rain dance, which is performed annually in the summer in conjunction with the harvesting of the cactus fruit, brings greening and ripening to the crops. A special drink is made from the cactus fruit called navait (nah-VITE). The Tohono O'odham drinks as much of this sacred wine as he can, just as the earth drinks rain that falls from the sky.

© Copyright 2000 Gary Braman

One of the memories I have of my family and grandparents is [of taking] trips to go pick materials I needed for my baskets. . . . [It has taken] me seventeen years to get to where I am now. I'm still learning. But over the seventeen years I've earned my patience. A lot of people always say, 'This [basket weaving] must take a lot of patience,' and my response is, 'You earn patience over the years.'

TERROL JOHNSON, TOHONO O'ODHAM

THE TRADITION CONTINUES

BARBARA YAZZIE, NAVAJO RUG WEAVER

© Copyright 1999 Arlette N. Braman

Barbara Yazzie, who lives on the Navajo reservation in northeastern Arizona, weaves beautiful rugs on a huge loom that stands upright in her living room. She weaves whenever she finds spare moments, supporting her family by selling her rugs. She can weave a rug in about a month if she has few interruptions. Barbara learned traditional weaving at the age of seven from her grandmother, who always had two looms—one for herself and a smaller one for Barbara. Barbara uses materials from the environment to dye her wool. Boiled walnut shells for brown, cedar bark for dark red, sagebrush for lime green, and ground white clay for a very bright white. Black comes from black sheep's wool.

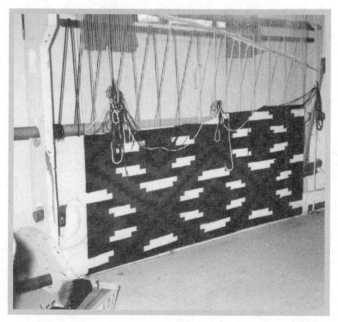

© Copyright 1999 Arlette N. Braman

"I remember a long time ago, my grandmother and aunties would gather together on the weekend. . . . They used to dump out a big bag of wool and then we'd be cleaning and carding it . . . and my grandmother and aunties would dry it."

BARBARA YAZZIE, NAVAJO RUG WEAVER

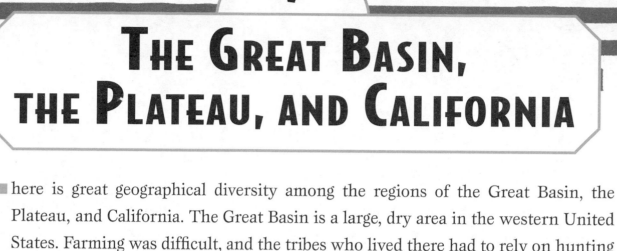

The Great Basin, the Plateau, and California

T here is great geographical diversity among the regions of the Great Basin, the Plateau, and California. The Great Basin is a large, dry area in the western United States. Farming was difficult, and the tribes who lived there had to rely on hunting and gathering plant foods, such as berries, wild onions, mesquite beans, carrots, and **piñons** (the edible seeds of a low-growing pine). Instead of creating permanent settlements, tribes would travel to where the best hunting and gathering spots were at the moment. Sacajawea, a Shoshone woman, served as a guide to Meriwether Lewis and William Clark, who were sent by the U.S. government on the first land expedition to the Pacific coast in 1804. Some of the nations today in this region include Bannock, Paiute, Shoshone, and Ute.

The plateau region consists of mountains, canyons, river valleys, and a dry **plateau** (a large area of land that has a relatively level surface raised above surrounding land). It includes areas of what are now Washington, Oregon, Idaho, and British Columbia,

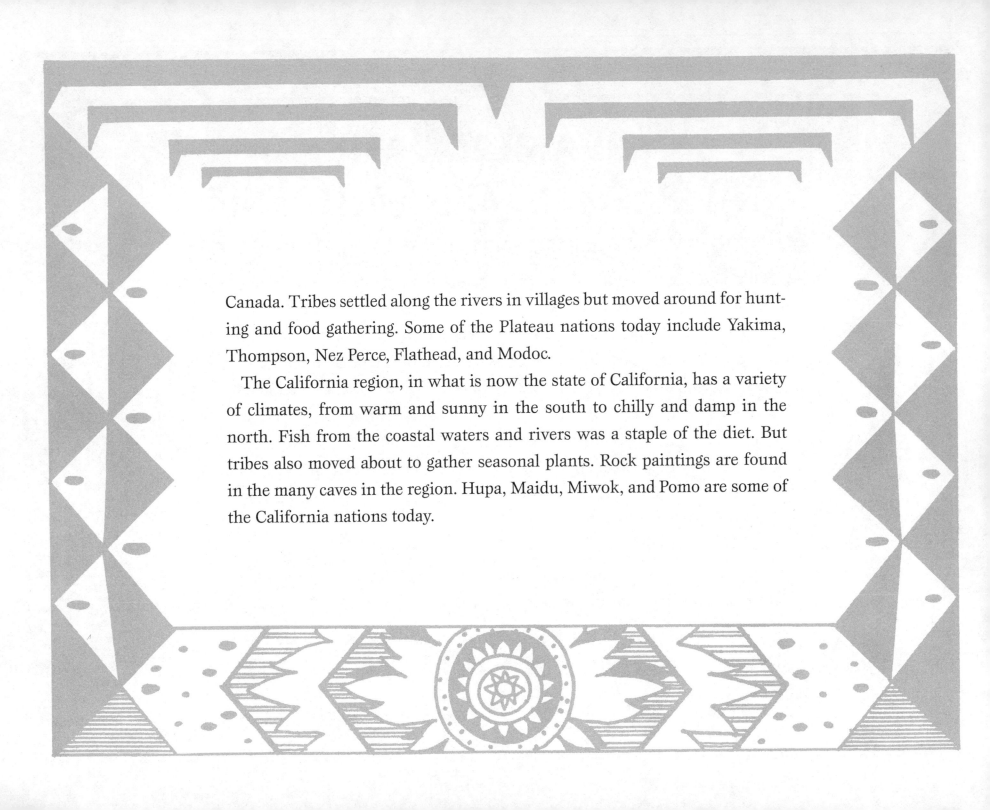

Canada. Tribes settled along the rivers in villages but moved around for hunting and food gathering. Some of the Plateau nations today include Yakima, Thompson, Nez Perce, Flathead, and Modoc.

The California region, in what is now the state of California, has a variety of climates, from warm and sunny in the south to chilly and damp in the north. Fish from the coastal waters and rivers was a staple of the diet. But tribes also moved about to gather seasonal plants. Rock paintings are found in the many caves in the region. Hupa, Maidu, Miwok, and Pomo are some of the California nations today.

Nez Perce 'Isaaptakay (Carrying Case)

The Nez Perce (nehz purs), the largest of the Plateau tribes, lived successfully for thousands of years on the almost 17 million acres (6.9 million ha) of their land in what is now Washington, Idaho, and Oregon. Before the 1800s, the Nez Perce moved about their land with the changing seasons to locate food. The high mountains, forests, and extensive river systems enabled the Nez Perce to gather edible plants, pick berries, dig for roots, hunt, and fish. They established villages and erected **semisubterranean** (partly underground) lodges covered with reeds. When they moved about, the Nez Perce erected cone-shaped, skin-covered tepees. They also erected longhouses, which were like long tepees.

NEZ PERCE TRADITION

The *qilloowawya* (kihl-O-wow-yah), or "serenade" as it was commonly known, was an ancient ceremony that was done when men had to travel to different parts of the country to hunt buffalo, trade with other tribes, harvest fish, or wage war. Everyone gathered around a rawhide and held it while singing songs and striking it with a stick. The men received gifts, including dried meat, small bags of roots, and an extra pair of moccasins for the journey. The word *qilloowawya* comes from two words: *qillilu*, which means "rawhide," and *wawya*, which means "to hit or strike."

During the 1850s, the U.S. government negotiated a number of treaties with the Nez Perce that granted them reservation lands from Oregon to Idaho. With the gold rush to this territory in 1863, the government took back about 6 million acres (2.4 million ha) of this reservation land, forcing the Nez Perce to live on a reservation in Idaho. Chief Joseph, a Nez Perce elder, refused to move his people, but he died before things could be settled. His son, Hin-mah-too-yah-lat-kekt, took his place. Called Joseph the Younger, he refused to move his band, and in 1877 General Oliver Otis Howard threatened to attack. Joseph reluctantly decided to move his people, but enraged warriors attacked white settlements and the army retaliated. Over three months, the band fought bravely

through an area that stretched 1,400 miles (2,253 km), but in 1877, Joseph surrendered. The Nez Perce were relocated first to Kansas, then to Oklahoma, before being allowed to return to Idaho. Today many Nez Perce live on these lands in north central Idaho, eastern Oregon, and Washington, and in British Columbia, Canada, and continue many of their traditional ways. The Nez Perce call themselves Nimiipuu (nih-MEE-poo), which means "People," and Cuupnitpeluu (TSOOP-nit-pah-loo), which means "People Emerging from the Mountain Forests."

> One time when I was fourteen or fifteen years old, I saw the old people trade their 'isaaptakay. They filled the 'isaaptakay with things unknown to the other people. When the time came to trade, they all exchanged their 'isaaptakay and opened [them] to see what they got. Nobody knew what they were getting, but they were always happy with what they received. . . . My grandma also used ['isaaptakay] to store dried fish and dried meat. She used the plain ones to store buckskin scraps so she would know what was in them. She had lots of them and . . . she knew which ones to look for.
>
> HORACE P. AXTELL, NEZ PERCE ELDER

Though not a Plains tribe, the Nez Perce often traveled east to hunt buffalo. They crafted a unique carrying case called an 'isaaptakay (ih-SOP-tuh-ki). The 'isaaptakay were unique because they were used to store and carry clothes and dried foods and were also used in "trade" ceremonies for births and marriages. For a marriage, the families of the bride and groom presented each other with trade items, including roots and meat, in the 'isaaptakay. The word, loosely translated, means "a covering or skin to pack things in." Traditionally, these carrying cases were made from the skins of animals, such as elk, buffalo, moose, and horse. The Nez Perce painted geometric designs on their 'isaaptakay, and the colors and designs had meaning to the person who made them. The designs often represented elements from oral stories. Some old, rare 'isaaptakay have **incised** (cut or marked with a sharp

instrument) designs. You can make an 'isaaptakay in the Nez Perce style to hold school papers, items you collect, or anything you like.

Here's What You Do

1 Mark a line 4 inches (10 cm) from each long edge of the poster board, and fold on the line.

2 Mark a line 8 inches (20 cm) from one short edge and fold. Mark a line 7 inches (18 cm) from the other short edge and fold. These are the flaps. When folded, the longer flap lies over the shorter flap. Use the hole punch to make two holes in each flap through both layers of poster board as shown, 8 inches (21 cm) apart and about 1 inch (2.5 cm) in from the edge of each flap. The holes should line up when the flaps are closed.

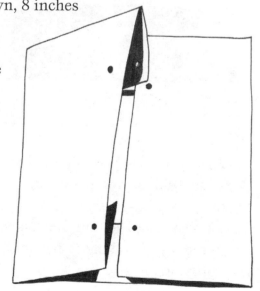

Fold over on all four edges of poster board

Punch holes in each flap through both layers of poster board

Here's What You Need

- [ ] pencil
- [ ] ruler
- [ ] sheet of white poster board, 28 by 22 inches (71 by 56 cm)
- [ ] one-hole punch
- [ ] craft paintbrush
- [ ] acrylic paints in green, blue, red, yellow, brown, and white
- [ ] small bowl of water
- [ ] paper towel
- [ ] yarn, string, or old shoelace, about 48 inches (122 cm) long

3 Unfold the *'isaaptakay* and lay it flat on your work surface, outside folds faceup. Lightly draw geometric designs on the poster board. Choose some Nez Perce designs like the ones shown or create your own.

Nez Perce Designs

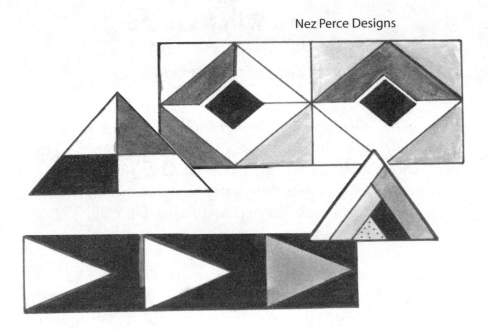

4 Paint your designs. Since *'isaaptakay* were made from animal skins, you might want to paint the background of the poster board a tan color. Mix a little brown paint with white paint to get tan. Remember to swish the paintbrush in the water and pat it dry on a paper towel before changing colors.

5 Let your *'isaaptakay* dry completely. To make a closure, thread the yarn through the holes and tie.

© Copyright 2000 Gary Braman

"My grandfather used to qilloowawya *quite a bit in his younger days. He knew quite a few songs from the ceremonies. He liked to wake up early in the morning and sing songs just so he could remember them. He would sing every morning, and each song was for a different event or reason."*

Josiah Blackeagle Pinkham, Nez Perce

Chumash Ring-and-Stick Game

The Chumash (CHOO-mahsh and also SHOO-mahsh) originally lived in what is now southern California for thousands of years and adapted well to this diverse landscape. Those who lived in the mountainous interior region hunted bear, fox, cougar, coyote, and quail, and gathered foods such as berries, nuts, seeds, and roots. The coastal and Channel Island Chumash were expert fishermen, enjoying a diet of fish and shellfish, seal, sea otter, and whale. Acorns were an important part of the Chumash diet. The Chumash were able to remove the toxins and bitter taste from this nut to create flour, acorn paste, acorn porridge, and acorn soup. The Chumash covered their dome-shaped homes, or 'aps (ahps), with **bulrush** (a marsh plant that grows in wetlands) and used willow and sycamore poles for the frames. A large whale rib was used for the arched doorway. The people who lived around the water designed plank canoes, called *tomol,* from driftwood that they split into planks. Owning one of these oceangoing vessels was a mark of great achievement.

CHUMASH TRADITION

Chumash men carved miniature canoes from **soapstone** (a soft metamorphic rock made up mostly of talc) and brought them on fishing excursions as charms to help ensure a good catch. These charms were buried with the owner, since it was believed that only the owner would know how to use the charm.

At one time, the Chumash were one of the largest of the California tribes. The establishment of missions in the 1700s brought settlers and disease, which drastically reduced the population. Today the Chumash number in the thousands and belong to a number of different bands and organizations living on some of their original homelands. Some of the bands in California today include the Santa Ynez reservation, the Coastal band of the Chumash Nation, the San Luis Obispo Chumash, the Ventura Chumash, and the Kern County Chumash.

The Chumash enjoyed playing games of skill, such as kickball, and games of chance, such as walnut-shell dice. Games of chance were believed to have religious significance, placing a great deal of importance on the supernatural. Gambling was an important part of both types of games. People would bet strings of shell-bead money and sometimes even their prized possessions on the outcome of a game. The

Each Chumash village had an area that was made into a playground by smoothing the ground and building a low wall around the area. A fun game of skill, the ring-and-stick game is easy to make but not so easy to play. If you have great hand-eye coordination, you'll soon be a pro at this Chumash game.*

Here's What You Need

- stick about 9 inches (23 cm) long and about as thick as a pencil
- piece of string or yarn about 20 inches (51 cm) long
- ring* with a 1-inch (2.5-cm) diameter

*You can find wooden or plastic rings at craft, hardware, or discount stores. Or look around your house for an old key ring, or any round object with an open center.

*Description of the ring-and-stick game from *Chumash Indian Games* by Travis Hudson and Jan Timbrook, copyright 1980. Used with permission.

Here's What You Do

1 Find a stick that has fallen from a tree in your backyard, a park, or anywhere outside. *Do not break a stick off a tree.*

2 Tie one end of the string to one end of the stick, then tie the other end of the string to the ring.

3 To play the game, hold the stick, toss the ring in the air, and try to catch the ring on the end of the stick. If you play with friends, keep score. Each time someone catches the ring on the stick, he or she scores a point. The player with the most points after 5 minutes is the winner!

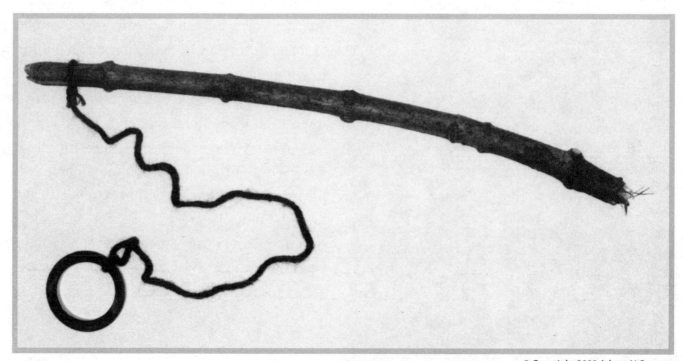

THE TRADITION CONTINUES

KEVIN PETERS, NEZ PERCE FLUTE MAKER

The art of Native American flute making and playing dates back thousands of years. In the Nez Perce language, the word for flute is *sepuunme's* (sah-POON-mahs). To Kevin Peters, the flute represents another voice and another way to communicate. Kevin taught himself how to make flutes, but he learned about the flute from Nez Perce elders. When Kevin makes a flute, he usually starts with a piece of elderberry wood and hollows out the inside by removing the **pith** (a soft, spongelike substance in the center of the stems and branches). This creates a nice, hollow tube that he can carve and smooth into an extraordinary flute. Kevin also teaches classes in traditional flute making to help continue the traditional ways of his people. Kevin believes that people everywhere enjoy flute music, and he feels the flutes he creates will have a lifelong relationship with him. In addition to making flutes, Kevin creates traditional art through his paintings and beadwork. Kevin does most of his own beadwork for the ceremonial outfit he wears for traditional dances.

> " *The love of arts* is *the love of life.* "
>
> KEVIN PETERS, NEZ PERCE FLUTE MAKER

VI

THE NORTHWEST COAST

From what is now southern Alaska through British Columbia, Canada, and into northern California, many nations thrived in the environment of the Northwest coast. The waters provided abundant fish, shellfish, and sea mammals. Forests supplied people with trees for building plank houses and carving canoes and totem poles. Many tribes traveled the rivers in canoes, trading extensively with their neighbors.

Since food was always plentiful, the people had more time to spend on decorative arts. The Bella Coola carved exquisite masks, the Makah wove baskets and mats, the Kwakiutl carved canoes, and the Haida made ceremonial dance capes with buttons made from **mother-of-pearl** (a hard, pearly, rainbow-colored substance lining the inside of an oyster shell or similar shellfish). Totem poles, a distinctive feature of this region, were carved from cedar logs and were originally meant to represent a family's social rank. Potlatches, social events held to show a

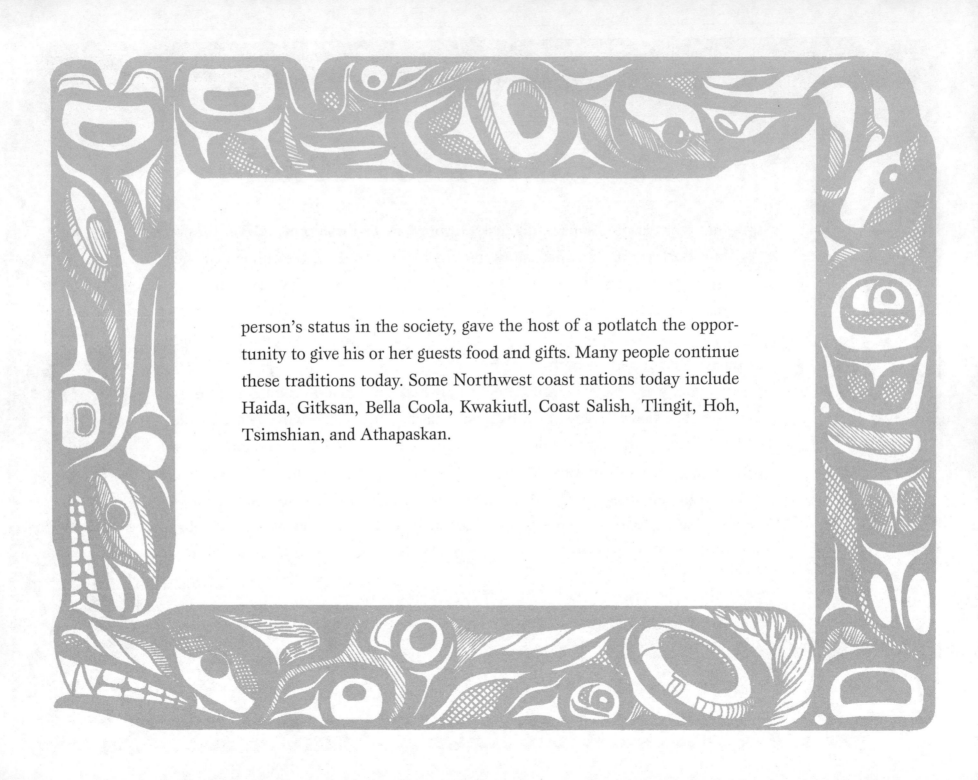

person's status in the society, gave the host of a potlatch the opportunity to give his or her guests food and gifts. Many people continue these traditions today. Some Northwest coast nations today include Haida, Gitksan, Bella Coola, Kwakiutl, Coast Salish, Tlingit, Hoh, Tsimshian, and Athapaskan.

Tlingit Button Blanket

Along the coast of what is now southeast Alaska and British Columbia, Canada, the Tlingit (TLIN-ghit) made their living off the land and sea. The forests gave them cedar wood for building long plank houses, wild game for food, and many varieties of wild berries. The Pacific Ocean provided them with fish and sea mammals. They gathered a variety of foods throughout the seasons and "put up" or preserved these foods for winter by drying, freezing, smoking, and more recently, canning. The Tlingit were wonderful artists and skilled navigators, who sometimes rigged their boats with sails made from tanned moose hides. They traveled the coast extensively for trade, to visit with other native peoples, for feasts and celebrations, and for potlatches. Today many Tlingit continue to live in traditional ways.

TLINGIT TRADITION

Button blankets, or ceremonial robes, are a very important part of many ceremonies. When an elder is presented with a button blanket to wear during a ceremony, the blanket gets named, which means that everyone acknowledges its importance. Ceremonial wear, such as button blankets, are always put away after the ceremony and are never displayed.

Before the Russian and European explorers, trappers, surveyors, and missionaries arrived in the area in the eighteenth century, the Tlingit way of life remained unchanged from that of their ancestors. With the discovery of gold in Alaska in 1896 came a flood of prospectors. Soon outsiders wanted more furs and gold and continued to move in, taking land away from the Tlingit. In 1971, Tlingit tribes received money and land with the passage of the Alaska Native Claims Settlement Act. The Tlingit today live in Alaska, Washington, Oregon, and British Columbia, Canada. Their name, *Tlingit,* means "the Tides People" or "People of the Tides."

The Tlingit are well known for making **button blankets** (ceremonial robes). The robes bear a crest design of the wearer's animal clan. In the Tlingit society, you are born into a clan and people know where you are from by your clan crest. The main clans are Eagle, with the subclans of Wolf,

Killer Whale, Bear, Thunderbird, and Raven, with the subclans of Beaver, Coho Salmon, and Sea Otter. Traditionally, the robes were made with red wool that was hand sewn on a solid blue or black background. Today the Tlingit also use fabrics such as fleece, cotton, and cashmere. Before the white settlers arrived in the 1700s, the Tlingit made buttons from the shells of **abalone** (an oysterlike shellfish with a flattened shell) or **dentalia** (varieties of tooth shells) to use as decoration on the robes. Later they used mother-of-pearl buttons that they got through trade. You can make a smaller version of a button blanket from felt and design a crest of an animal that best represents you.

Here's What You Need

- [ ] pencil
- [ ] scrap paper
- [ ] scissors
- [ ] 2 pieces of felt, one blue and one red, $^3/_4$ yard (68.5 cm) each
- [ ] ruler
- [ ] fabric glue
- [ ] chalk

- [ ] about 70 to 80 buttons,* $^1/_4$ to $^1/_2$ inch (.5 to 1 cm) in diameter
- [ ] thick craft glue
- [ ] needle
- [ ] thread

* Look for old buttons around your house or at flea markets, or ask friends for some.

Here's What You Do

1 Think about an animal that best represents you to use as your crest. If you love to swim, you might want to draw a fish. Or if you live in the mountains, maybe draw a bear. Practice drawing on the scrap paper your animal crest and any designs you want to use on your blanket. Some sample animal crests are shown here.

fish

bear

raven

2 Cut a piece of blue felt that measures 14 by 17 inches (35.5 by 43 cm). Set it aside. Cut a piece of red felt that measures 12 by 13 inches (30.5 by 33 cm).

3 Center the red piece of felt over the blue piece, lining up the bottom edges. You should have about a 2-inch (5-cm) blue border on the top, left, and right edges. Glue the red piece of felt in place, using the fabric glue.

4 Lightly draw your animal crest design on the leftover blue felt, using chalk. Cut out the design and place it in the red felt area of your blanket anyway you think it will look best. Then glue it in place.

5 While the felt is drying, draw some designs for the border of your blanket on the leftover red felt in chalk. Cut these out and place them around the border until you like your design. Glue each cutout design in place on the border.

Glue designs around border

Glue animal crest design in center

6 You may want to add some design details on your animal crest and on the edge of the red felt area as shown here. These can be done using felt or buttons. When gluing buttons to fabric, put small dots of *thick craft glue* on the back of the button and lightly press the button in place.

7 Glue buttons around the left, right, and top edges of the red felt. Line up the buttonholes so they form a straight line. Let the glue dry completely.

8 Thread the needle and sew the buttons on the blanket. Starting at one end of the row of buttons, push the needle up through one of the holes in the button and down through the opposite hole in the same button. Then push the needle up and down through the pair of holes in the next button.

Stitch around outside entire crest design

Glue on design details

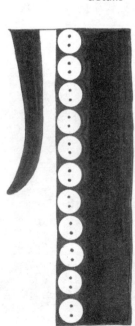

Line up buttonholes so they form a straight line

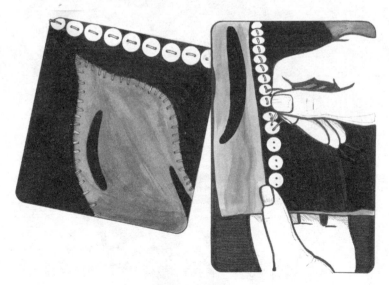

Push needle up through one buttonhole, then down through opposite hole

9 Continue sewing until all the buttons have been sewn on the blanket. Then stitch around the outside of the entire crest design. Hang your button blanket in your room.

© Copyright 2000 Gary Braman

One of the strongest beliefs that we of the Tlingit people have still to this day is our connection, our being related to the animals of the Northwest coast. This is part of why we take on a certain totem, or crest of the animal.

CLARISSA HUDSON, TLINGIT

Hoh Fry Bread

The Hoh (ho) have always lived in northwest Washington. Because of their location, where the mouth of the Hoh River meets the Pacific Ocean, the Hoh became expert navigators, traveling river and coastal routes to reach fishing locations, hunting grounds, other villages, and places for harvesting plants. Carvers split a cedar tree in half to make two canoes. Small trees were used for racing canoes, medium trees for river canoes, and large trees for oceangoing vessels. They "paddled" their canoes to attend potlatches. Wood from the cedar trees was also used to make their longhouses, carved totem poles, and much more. Today many of the Hoh tribal members continue traditions that have been handed down from generation to generation.

The earliest European explorations of this area probably occurred in the sixteenth century. The 1700s brought more white settlers and fur trappers to the area, and in 1893, the U.S. government set aside about 443 acres (179 ha) of reservation land for the Hoh. Hoh men try to make a living by fishing, but it does not support a family. The tribal office employs people, as does the fishery. The Hoh call themselves Cha'laat (chah-lot), which means "the Ones Who Live on the Hoh."

HOH TRADITION

The Hoh hold a ceremony when a child is given a Native American name, called a name-giving potlatch. Many tribes are invited and travel far distances to attend. The child receiving the name is introduced to everyone and the people are told which member of the child's family is giving the name. Some guests receive handkerchiefs with silver dollars in them, and from then on they must say the child's Native American name and ask how he or she is whenever they see the child. Each family sings songs unique to itself, with the tribe who traveled the farthest going first. As a way of honoring the guests, the host family provides food and gives gifts.

The river and coastal areas also provided food such as salmon, seafood, and seal. The forests yielded elk, deer, and many types of wild berries. Many Hoh today continue to fish

and hunt these animals. Berry picking is popular, and some of the favorites include strawberries, salmonberries, and blackberries, which are harvested and eaten fresh or canned for later use. Homemade huckleberry jam is spread on fry bread, another favorite food. These individual breads are easy to make and are so delicious it's impossible to eat just one!*

Here's What You Need

SERVINGS: 8 SMALL OR 4 LARGE LOAVES
Recipe requires adult help.

Ingredients
- 2 cups (480 ml) flour
- 2 tablespoons (30 ml) baking powder
- 1 teaspoon (5 ml) salt
- 2 tablespoons (30 ml) dry milk
- 1 cup (240 ml) lukewarm water
- vegetable oil
- huckleberry jam*

*If you can't find huckleberry jam, choose a berry jam you like.

Equipment
- wooden spoon
- measuring cup
- measuring spoons
- large bowl
- large frying pan
- paper towel
- plate
- slotted spoon
- butter knife

*Recipe from Viola Riebe. Used with permission.

Here's What You Do

1 Use the wooden spoon to mix all the ingredients in the bowl. Generously sprinkle a clean, flat surface with flour, place the dough on the surface, and **knead** (squeeze, press, or roll with the hands) the dough about 3 minutes. You will need to sprinkle additional flour over the dough and on your hands as you work.

2 Shape the dough into about eight small or four large balls. Use your fingers to flatten each ball to a thickness of about ¼ inch (.5 cm), and set them aside on the work surface until all of the balls are flattened. The loaf shapes may vary, but this is fine.

3 Pour the oil in the frying to a depth of about ½ inch (1 cm) and heat the oil on medium-high for a few minutes. Cover the plate with the paper towel and set it aside.

Shape dough into balls, then flatten to ¼ inch (.5 cm) thick

4 *Ask an adult* to help you fry the flattened loaves on one side until lightly browned, then use the slotted spoon to carefully turn each loaf and brown lightly on the other side. The loaves brown quickly, so watch them carefully. Lower the heat to medium if the oil gets too hot. Transfer the lightly browned loaves to the plate covered with the paper towel, using the slotted spoon. Let the fry bread cool slightly, then use the butter knife to spread on
your favorite jam.
Eat and enjoy!

> *With all the changes in technology, we have maintained our customs and traditions that have been handed down or taught by our elders.*
>
> VIOLA RIEBE, HOH

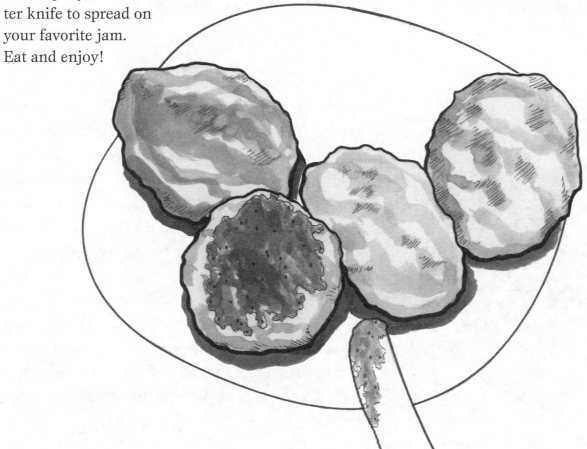

HOH FRY BREAD   **91**

Tsimshian Life Crest

The Tsimshian (SIHM-shee-in) lived along the banks of the Skeena and Nass Rivers in British Columbia, Canada. The Tsimshian who lived near the coast depended more on fishing halibut, seal, sea otter, and sea lions, while the Tsimshian who lived inland hunted bear and mountain goats. They all depended on salmon, an important food in their diet. Along the beach, they built large wooden homes with painted crests on the front. The Tsimshian developed friendly relations with many of their neighbors and became skilled traders, exchanging fish oil for carved Haida canoes and fur from inland subarctic tribes. They excelled in the art of painting and carving, creating dramatic totems that displayed family crests and myths of ancestral achievements. Today many Tsimshian are reviving the traditional ways of their people.

TSIMSHIAN TRADITION

The Tsimshian maintain a strong love and respect for nature and all living things because these things are believed to be gifts from the Creator.

The Tsimshian have lived in the area for more than 5,000 years, and life remained stable and unchanged until the arrival of Europeans in the late 1700s. Many Tsimshian continue to make their home in British Columbia, Canada, on reservation lands. Their original name, Cmsyan (SIM-shan), means "People inside the Skeena River."

Crests representing animals of the Pacific Northwest coast are important symbols in the Tsimshian clan society. The four main clans are the Killer Whale (or Blackfish), the Raven, the Eagle, and the Wolf, with subclans for each. You are born into a clan and the crest becomes your life crest because you keep it for life. Traditionally, children inherit their mother's clan and the crest that is owned by the clan. Crests are passed down from one generation to the next. They are painted, carved, and sewn on many items, such as drums, dishes, storage boxes, canoes, ceremonial dress, housefront paintings, and totem poles. In this project, you will select a Tsimshian crest that best represents you and paint it on a piece of wood in the Tsimshian style.

Here's What You Need

- piece of scrap wood,* about 7 by 5 inches (18 by 13 cm)
- sandpaper, fine grain
- tack rag** or a *slightly damp* rag
- pencil
- craft paintbrush
- acrylic paint, black
- acrylic spray sealer (optional—requires adult help)

* If you can't find a piece of scrap wood around your house, ask a lumberyard or home improvement center for a piece of scrap wood.

** A tack rag is a sticky rag used to wipe dust off wood and can be bought at any hardware store.

Here's What You Do

1 Read the crest characteristics shown on the following page. Then choose one that best fits you. That will be your life crest.

3 In pencil, lightly draw the animal crest you've selected on the surface of the wood.

4 Paint your animal crest in black paint, leaving some spaces unpainted, as in the sample crests.

Killer Whale
kind, family spirit, strong, aggressive

Otter
fun-loving, ambitious, kind, giving, creative

Frog
wise, patient, well-spoken

Hummingbird
gentle, joyful, messenger of love, healing spirit, musical

Paint your animal crest in black

SALMON
Survival
Loves water

2 Don't worry if your piece of wood is not a perfect rectangle. Odd shapes are more interesting. Sand the piece of wood until the surface and edges feel smooth. Wipe the dust off, using the tack rag. If using a damp rag, let the piece of wood dry completely.

5 Let the painted wood dry completely. Lightly spray the painted surface with the acrylic sealer, if you want. *Do this outside with the help of an adult.* When the sealer is dry, you can use your life crest as a bookend, a paperweight, or just as a decoration.

" *I was always intrigued by the stories my granny Helin used to tell. She was always encouraging me to learn traditions and, most importantly, the art forms, so as to pass them on to future generations [and not let them] die.* "

BILL HELIN, TSIMSHIAN

THE TRADITION CONTINUES

CLARISSA HUDSON, TLINGIT ARTIST

Clarissa Hudson works hard to continue the traditions of her people. She makes button blankets, which are used as ceremonial robes, creating her own designs. Clarissa, a member of the Raven clan and the T'ak Dein Taan subclan, was born and raised in Alaska. She learned the art of **Chilkat** (weaving style of the Chilkat Tlingit) weaving from the late Jennie Thlunaut of Klukwan, Alaska, the last of the traditional Chilkat weavers, and attended the Institute of American Indian Arts in Sante Fe, New Mexico, to further hone her craft. She helps aspiring weavers develop and refine this art by offering monthlong apprenticeships. Since she studied in the Southwest and makes her home there, some of her original designs incorporate a subtle Southwestern influence. Clarissa occasionally conducts workshops in Alaska, which gives her an opportunity to visit with family and enjoy activities from her childhood, such as fishing and berry picking.

"Thunderbird Mother" copyright © 1999 by Clarissa Hudson. Used with permission.

"*I have chosen ceremonial robes as my medium for portraying dreams, visions, and interpretations of personal experiences. It is my medicine.*"

CLARISSA HUDSON, TLINGIT ARTIST

96

VII
THE SUBARCTIC AND ARCTIC

The subarctic region includes a large portion of Canada and Alaska. Pine and birch forests, called **taiga,** cover most of the region. Though the winters are cold, the area is not completely snow-covered and does thaw in the spring, except for the **tundra** (a treeless plain that has black, mucky soil and a permanently frozen subsoil), which remains frozen. Native peoples moved about as the seasons changed. The Ingalik moved to temporary camps near good fishing sites in spring. Other groups moved to the mountains in early winter to hunt caribou. The coast provided native peoples with sea mammals, and the rivers supplied salmon and other fish. Winter homes of the Ingalik were built into the earth and had roofs of poles and beams onto which mats were placed. The Cree and Ojibwa constructed conical lodges with roofs of tree boughs, earth, and snow. These ingenious people created wooden toboggans, snowshoes, and snow goggles to protect their eyes against the bright sun. Subarctic nations today include Cree, Carrier, Kutchin, Ingalik, and Beaver.

The Arctic region extends from the Bering Sea to Greenland. The region remains snow-covered all winter. The Inuit (IN-oo-it) make their home here. The Inuit traditionally lived a subsistence lifestyle, which means they acquired only what they needed to survive by hunting, fishing, and gathering. They moved about with the seasons but were not nomadic, since they returned to the same areas each year. Their dwellings in summer were animal-hide tents and in winter they constructed round sections of structures covered with skins and blocks of **sod** (the grass-covered surface of the ground). The Canadian Central Inuit sometimes constructed temporary iglus of ice blocks to use as hunting lodges. The word *iglu* is Inuit for *house,* and iglus were more frequently hide- or sod-covered dome-shaped homes. Today many Inuit combine their traditional lifestyle with modern technology. Snowmobiles and all-terrain vehicles have replaced dogsleds, though some Inuit who live in remote areas still rely on dogsleds for transportation.

The Aleut (uh-LOOT) also made their home in the Arctic region in the Aleutian Islands. They lived a subsistence lifestyle, depending on hunting, fishing, and gathering. Their homes, called barabaras, were constructed partly underground and had a sod-covered roof. The Aleut today continue many of their traditional ways.

The Arctic people are the Aleut, or Unangan, their original name, which means "the People," and the Inuit, which also means "the People," as well as the Yupik, Inupiat, Labrador Coast Inuit, Copper Inuit, Bering Strait Inuit, East and West Greenland Inuit, and Iglulik.

Cree Moccasins

For thousands of years, the Cree (kree) lived in various parts of what is now Canada. They survived by hunting animals, such as moose, caribou, and bear, trapping beaver and muskrat, and fishing in the many lakes and rivers for whitefish, pike, and trout. The Cree established villages, constructing wigwams made from wooden poles set in the shape of a cone, over which bark, animal hides, and moss were placed. In the winter, many Cree traveled by dogsled or toboggan over the snowy terrain or used snowshoes for walking. During summer, they traveled in birch-bark canoes and were excellent navigators. Pemmican, made from dried meat that had been pounded into a powder, mixed with animal fat and cranberries, and stuffed into animals' intestines, was a favorite food.

CREE TRADITION

Every August, the Opaskwayak Cree Nation hosts the Indian Days Festival in northern Manitoba, Canada. Events such as goose and moose calling and canoe racing are favorites. Cree and tourists alike enjoy traditional foods, including moose stew and **bannock** (a flat bread or biscuit made with oatmeal or barley meal). The nation is located where bands have gathered traditionally throughout history to hunt, socialize, and practice spiritual life.

Around the mid-1600s, white fur traders arrived on Cree lands in search of beaver pelts. The Cree showed the fur traders how to survive in this environment and often worked in partnership with them. The demand for pelts increased, attracting more people to western Canada. But with overtrapping, beaver and other wildlife became scarce and many newcomers turned their attention to agriculture. Because of this, the Cree lost more of their land. They had to move their villages many times until they finally entered into treaties with the British (Canada was a colony of Great Britain) and received reservations. Today the Cree nation consists of many different communities, or bands, located throughout Canada, who continue many of their traditional ways. Their own name, Anishinabe (ah-NISH-ih-NA-bey) means "First People."

The Cree have always crafted useful and decorative items, including birch-bark baskets and clothing made from animal skins. Before European contact, items such as moccasins,

Here's What You Need

- ☐ piece of paper, 8½ by 11 inches (21.5 by 28 cm)*
- ☐ ruler
- ☐ pencil
- ☐ scissors
- ☐ two 12-by-17-inch (30.5-by-43-cm) pieces of felt, in tan if you want it to resemble an animal hide, or any color you'd like**
- ☐ straight pins
- ☐ chalk
- ☐ embroidery needle or sewing needle with large eye
- ☐ embroidery floss in a variety of colors
- ☐ thread in a color to match your moccasins
- ☐ nonskid pads***

* If you have a big foot, use a larger piece of paper.

** Use felt that is sold by the bolt.

*** You can find nonskid pads in any fabric or craft store, or in the craft section of discount stores, such as Kmart or Wal-Mart.

pouches, and clothing were decorated with floral designs made from beads and porcupine quills. After European contact, women received thread through trade and used **embroidery** (decorative needlework) on items such as moccasins. The word *moccasin* comes from the Cree word *makisinuk* (mah-kuh-see-NUHK), which means "shoes." Cree women made moccasins from moose or caribou hides. There were many different moccasin styles. The hard-soled kind, better suited for the Plains Cree, protected their feet from rocks and prairie grass. The soft-soled type of moccasin worked better for woodland and some Plains tribes. Moccasin styles and designs were so unique that a person could tell the tribe of the wearer just by looking at the mocassin, and even by a footprint left behind in the ground. You can make a pair of felt moccasins in the Cree style with an embroidered floral design.

Here's What You Do

1 Put the paper on the ground and place your right foot on top of it. Your foot needs to be 2 inches (5 cm) in from the right edge of the paper. With the pencil, mark the paper 1 inch (2.5 cm) from the tip of your longest toe. Mark 1 inch (2.5 cm) to the left of the widest part of your foot, and 1 inch (2.5 cm) below your heel.

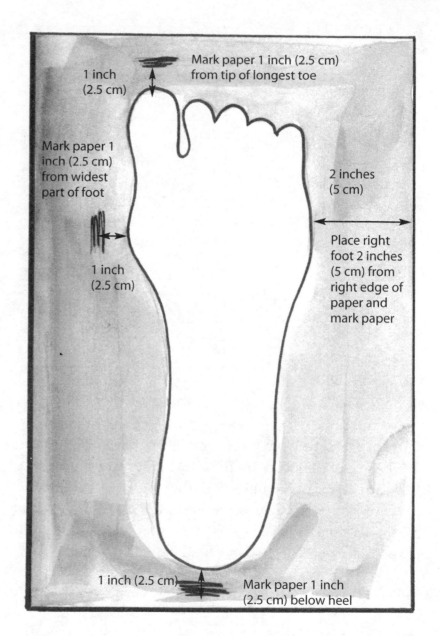

1 inch (2.5 cm)

Mark paper 1 inch (2.5 cm) from tip of longest toe

Mark paper 1 inch (2.5 cm) from widest part of foot

2 inches (5 cm)

1 inch (2.5 cm)

Place right foot 2 inches (5 cm) from right edge of paper and mark paper

1 inch (2.5 cm)

Mark paper 1 inch (2.5 cm) below heel

2 Draw lines as shown to connect your marks. This is the pattern for your moccasins. Cut out the pattern along the lines.

3 Fold one piece of felt in half, short edges together. Place the paper moccasin pattern on top of the folded piece of felt. Line up the right, straight edge of the pattern with the folded edge of the felt, then pin the

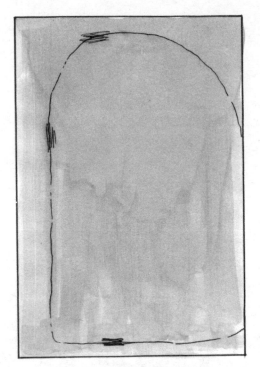

Draw lines to connect marks, then cut along lines

paper to both layers of the felt. Using the chalk, trace the outline of the paper on the felt. This is your first moccasin. Remove the pins and paper from the felt, pin the felt together again, then cut out the felt outline, keeping the felt folded as you cut. Repeat this step with the second piece of felt for the second moccasin.

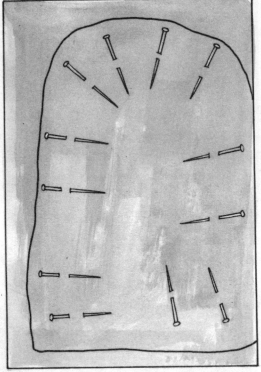

fold

Trace outline of pattern on felt with chalk

Line up right edge of pattern with folded edge, then pin pattern to both layers of felt

4 Open one cutout felt moccasin and lay it flat on your work surface. The crease or fold should be down the middle (the sole of the moccasin). Using the chalk, lightly draw the traditional Cree design on the felt near both outside edges as shown here. Repeat this step for the other cutout felt moccasin.

each stitch lines up with the previous one. Do not pull the stitches too tightly or the felt will bunch up. Embroider the entire design, changing colors whenever you like.

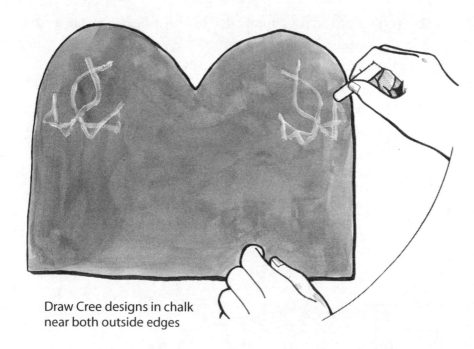

Draw Cree designs in chalk near both outside edges

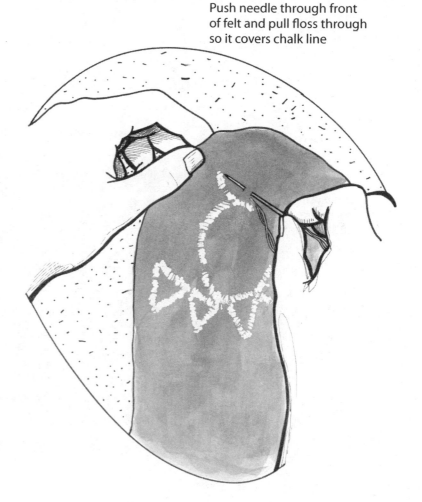

Push needle through front of felt and pull floss through so it covers chalk line

5 Use the embroidery floss to embroider the design on both moccasins. To embroider, thread the needle with embroidery floss and knot the end of one strand. Push the needle up through the back of the felt (the side without the chalk design) along the left edge of the chalk line and pull the floss all the way through. Then for each stitch, push the needle from right to left through the front of the felt (with the chalk design) and pull the floss through so that it covers the chalk line. Continue in this way, making sure

6 Pin the right sides of one moccasin together so that the embroidered designs are on the *inside* of the moccasin. Sew the front, curved edge of the moccasin together, using a running stitch (see page 6). Slip your foot into the moccasin and pin the back, heel edges together so that the moccasin fits comfortably. Take the moccasin off and sew the back edges together, making your last stitch 1 inch (2.5 cm) from the top.

7 To gather the top, open edge of the moccasin, use a running stitch all the way around the top edge about ½ inch (1 cm) from the edge. Do not sew through both layers. Gently pull the floss to gather or pucker the edge. Sew over the last stitch on the inside of the moccasin three times to secure it, then cut the floss. Repeat steps 6 and 7 with the other moccasin.

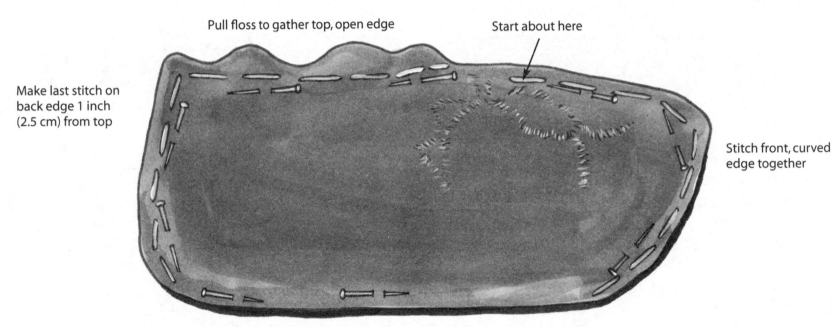

Pull floss to gather top, open edge

Start about here

Make last stitch on back edge 1 inch (2.5 cm) from top

Stitch front, curved edge together

Pin sides of moccasin together so embroidered design is on inside

8 Turn the moccasins right side out and try them on. Sew a small piece of the nonskid pad to the ball and heel surfaces of the sole of the moccasins.

Often hides were scarce. My mother would buy felt hats from the local mission or Salvation Army. She would make moccasins for all of us children.

LIONEL deMONTIGNY, CHIPPEWA CREE

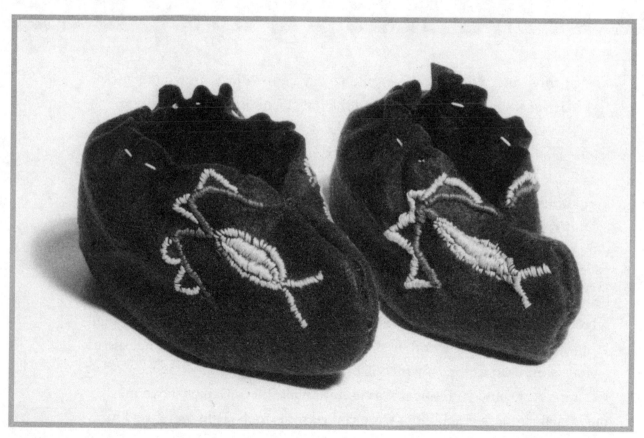

© Copyright 2000 Gary Braman

Yupik Wild Raspberry Dessert

For thousands of years, the Yupik have lived in villages in what is now Alaska along the Bering Sea and the lower Yukon and Kuskokwim Rivers. The Siberian Yupik have always lived on what is now Saint Lawrence Island in the Bering Sea. In earlier times, they traveled with the seasons, moving to temporary fishing camps in the warmer months to fish for king salmon, trout, and halibut. In the spring, they gathered smelt. The inland Yupik hunted moose and caribou. All gathered berries, birds' eggs, and wild plants, such as fiddleheads, wild celery, and wild parsley.

In addition to hunting polar bear, walrus, and seal, spring whaling has been a tradition with some Yupik, such as the Siberian Yupik. They hunted whales from **umiaks** (boats covered with animal skins that can hold a small group of people) and ate and used every part of the whale. They ate **muktuk** (whale skin used as food), which is **blubber** (fat) with skin attached, for vitamins A, D, and C. Blubber was used to make oil for lamps. Jawbones made sled runners. Backbones were carved into stools. Ribs were used for house rafters, and shoulder blades made handy snow shovels. Because of their somewhat remote location, many Yupik today continue to live in the traditional ways of their ancestors, but have also adopted modern ways.

In the 1700 and 1800s, fur trappers, miners, and whaling ships arrived in the area, taking control over native lands. When the United States purchased the territory of Alaska from Russia in 1867, the native peoples lost the rights to their land. But in 1971, the U.S. government passed the Alaska Native Claims Settlement Act and agreed to provide the native peoples with millions of dollars through the establishment of native-run corporations and title to millions of acres (hectares) of land. The Yupik represent the largest group of Alaskan natives. Many have jobs in schools, in government, and in stores, especially in the Hooper Bay area. Yupik means "the People."

Relying on food from the land and sea to survive has been a Yupik tradition for many years. Whether ice fishing in winter for cod, a delicious fish eaten with seal oil, or gathering wild plants in summer and fall, these traditions help maintain close family ties. Berry picking is a fun traditional family activity. Different kinds of berries ripen at different times. During June and July, blueberries and salmonberries ripen and are ready for picking. In August, you can still find salmonberries, and you can also harvest blackberries and cranberries. These delicious berries are eaten fresh, made into jams and jellies, or dried for later use. They are also mixed with other foods, such as lard and sugar, to make Eskimo ice cream. Another favorite is a dessert made from wild raspberries. You can make this easy Yupik dessert from *The Togiak School Cookbook* whenever you're in the mood for a delicious treat.*

Here's What You Need

SERVINGS: 2

Ingredients

- [ ] 2 cups (450 ml) wild raspberries*
- [ ] ¼ cup (56 ml) sugar
- [ ] 1 tablespoon (15 ml) canned evaporated milk

*If you can't find wild raspberries where you live, you can buy raspberries at the supermarket. Or you can use blueberries. *Always check with an adult before picking or eating any wild berries.*

Equipment

- [ ] measuring cup
- [ ] large bowl
- [ ] potato masher or large fork
- [ ] measuring spoons
- [ ] serving spoon
- [ ] 2 small bowls
- [ ] 2 spoons

*Recipe for Yupik Wild Raspberry Dessert reprinted from *The Togiak School Cookbook*. Used with permission of the author, Fran Shugak.

YUPIK TRADITION

During the summer months, Yupik women and girls enjoy telling stories with a story knife. The story is often combined with singing. They sit in a circle and one girl starts by smoothing the mud, using a knife carved from ivory, wood, or animal bone. As she begins her story, she draws pictures of her home and characters to set the stage for her story. When she is finished, the next girl begins her story. This form of storytelling helps preserve the Yupik way of life.

"Elitelleq Nangyuituq *(lee-DETH-uck NUNG-you-ee-dook). In the Yupik Eskimo language, it means 'learning is forever.'*"

Fanny Parker, Yupik

Here's What You Do

1 Place the berries in the bowl and mash with the potato masher or large fork.

2 Add the sugar and taste the berries. If you'd like them sweeter, add a little more sugar and stir.

3 Add the milk and stir.

4 Serve in the small bowls and enjoy!

Inupiat Games

For more than 10,000 years, the Inupiat (ih-NEE-OO-pee-aht) have made their home in an area that stretches from present-day Unalakeet on the western Alaskan coast below the Bering Strait to the Canadian border. In earlier times these Alaskan natives lived a subsistence lifestyle of hunting, fishing, and gathering, similar to that of their other native neighbors. Trapping rabbits for food and fur was common with some groups, while herding and hunting caribou or reindeer in winter was done by most, if it becomes necessary. Many communities gathered a variety of foods, such as fresh greens; duck and goose eggs; berries such as salmonberries, blueberries, and raspberries; and birch bark and tree roots for basket making. Hunting seal, walrus, moose, and bear for food and fur was important. Some communities shared similar seasonal activities, such as hunting the bowhead whale in the spring and fall, while others didn't hunt the whale at all. Today many Inupiat continue their traditional way of life.

INUPIAT TRADITION

The whaling festival is an important tradition of many Inupiat and is held in thanksgiving for a successful and safe season. In Barrow, Alaska, on the day of the festival, whale meat, tea, biscuits, and other foods are given to the guests throughout the day. Beginning at 10 o'clock in the morning, festival goers have fun tossing someone in a blanket made from hides of the bearded seal sewn together. Participants hold the roped edge of the blanket while tossing the person into the air. The object of the blanket toss game is for the person tossed to return to the blanket in an upright position. If you lose your balance, someone else gets a turn. Everyone gets a chance to participate. Members of a successful whaling crew hold bags of candy as they are being tossed, and onlookers enjoy catching the candy.* It is thought that the blanket toss , or *nalukataq,* originated because of the need to look out over distances for game. Being tossed afforded a long-distance view.

*Different Inupiat communities may play the game a little differently.

The Inupiat encountered the same problems as their neighbors when outsiders moved onto their ancestral homelands. The Inupiat also benefited from the Alaska Native Claims Settlement Act (see page 107). The many communities living in this region, the farthest north of any Alaskan natives, are very diverse. The name Inupiat means "Real People."

Like children everywhere, Inupiat children enjoy playing games. While Inupiat children enjoy electronic toys, basketball, soccer, and hockey, many traditional games continue to be played. In the bone puzzle game, a bunch of small bones, usually from a seal's hind flipper, are piled in a heap. When the signal is given, the players lay the bones out in a row and try to reconstruct the skeleton of the flipper. Another game, darts, is played by throwing a large dart, usually made from caribou antlers and bone that have been sharpened to a point, at a target on the ground. Cat's cradle, a string game played with the fingers, is fun but not always easy to master. You may have tried it yourself sometime. Two Inupiat games, *maq* (muhk) and *aakuu, aakuu* (AH-koo AH-koo), are played and enjoyed by both children and adults. The games require little or no equipment. You only need yourself and some friends.

Inupiat Maq

Here's What You Need

☐ 3 or more players

Here's What You Do

Object of the Game: To make the other players laugh

1 Gather everyone together and sit in a circle. One player is selected to begin the game.

2 The person selected must make the other players laugh by making faces or using body movements but is not allowed to make any noises. Whoever laughs first takes the next turn at trying to make the others laugh. You can continue playing until everyone has had a turn.

Inupiat Aakuu, Aakuu

Here's What You Need

- stick
- scarf or mitten
- 6 or more players

Here's What You Do

Object of the Game: To bring the opposing team members to your side

1 Select two team captains. One captain throws the stick in the air while the other captain catches it. The captains take turns moving their fists up the stick, hand over hand to the top of the stick. The first captain to reach the top of the stick picks his or her first team member. Then the captains take turns picking members until all players are on teams.

2 Both teams line up, facing each other and about 25 feet (8 m) apart. The winning captain's team goes first.

3 Team 1 decides which player to *aakuu* (bring over) from team 2. Waving the scarf or mitten, the team captain calls out, "*Aakuu, aakuu* (name of player) will come over while play acting an animal, person, or situation." Some examples include a bear, a wrestler, or ice fishing. While acting out his or her animal, person, or situation, the player must go to the captain of team 1, keeping a straight face. If the player smiles or laughs, he must join the *aakuu* side (team 1). If he makes it to the other side without laughing or smiling, he may take the scarf or mitten from the captain and go back to team 2. He can then try to *aakuu* a player from team 1 to team 2. The team with the most players wins.

> *Growing up I remember seining fish, picking berries, ice fishing, camping, mushing dogs, and gardening. . . . I love ice fishing and berry picking. . . . My favorite native foods are akutuk [Eskimo ice cream] made with salmonberries and blackberries, and white and black muktuk.*
>
> DARLENE C. "RED" SEEBERGER, INUPIAT

THE TRADITION CONTINUES

MATTIE JO AKLACHEAK AHGEAK, INUPIAT STUDENT

In many ways, Mattie Jo Aklacheak Ahgeak is like most other nine-year-old children. She is in the third grade at Ipalook Elementary School in Barrow, Alaska. She loves working on the computer, has to do her homework like other kids, and enjoys spending time with her three sisters and her parents, James and Mae Ahgeak. But Mattie Jo is unique in that she continues the traditional ways of her ancestors. She goes hunting with her family, which is a traditional Inupiat activity. In October, Mattie Jo also enjoys ice fishing, which she is doing in the photo shown here. She learned to ice fish from her mom and dad. It takes time and patience to ice fish, so Mattie Jo wears her warmest clothes and uses fishing tools such as a spear. After all her hard work, Mattie Jo is rewarded with enough fish to feed her family. One of her favorite native foods is whitefish. She likes to eat it frozen or cooked with seal oil.

"We go fishing to put food on our table.
MATTIE JO AKLACHEAK AHGEAK, INUPIAT

Glossary

abalone   An oysterlike shellfish with a flattened shell.

adobe   A sun-dried brick made of clay and straw.

appliqué   A cutout decoration attached or sewn to a larger piece of material for accent.

bannock   A flat bread or biscuit made with oatmeal or barley meal.

blubber   Fat.

bulrush   A marsh plant that grows in wetlands.

button blanket   A ceremonial robe.

calico   Cotton cloth with patterns.

Chilkat   A weaving style of the Chilkat Tlingit.

clan   A division or group within a tribe that is closely related.

coaster   A small mat used to protect a tabletop or other surface.

dentalia   Varieties of tooth shells.

embroidery   Decorative needlework.

finger weaving   Weaving done without a loom, using only the fingers.

incise   To cut into or mark with a sharp instrument.

kiln   An oven, furnace, or other heated enclosure used for processing an object by burning, firing, or drying.

knead   To squeeze, press, or roll a material such as dough with the hands.

loom   A frame for interlacing two or more threads or yarns to make cloth.

mother-of-pearl   A hard, pearly, rainbow-colored substance lining the inside of an oyster shell or similar shellfish.

muktuk   Whale skin used as food.

nation   A tribe or federation of tribes.

pack   To push down.

piñon   The edible seed of a low-growing pine.

pith   A soft, spongelike substance in the center of the stems and branches of a woody plant.

plateau   A large area of land that has a relatively level surface raised above surrounding land.

prospector   A person who explores an area for mineral deposits.

quillwork   Ornamentation of a hide for decorative purposes by applying porcupine quills in a variety of ways.

reservation   A tract of land set aside for use by a group of people.

roach   A headdress.

sapling   A small tree.

semisubterranean   Partly underground.

shackle   Something that confines the leg or arm.

slip   A mixture of finely ground clay and water applied over a pot with a brush, cloth, or piece of leather to smooth and/or color it.

soapstone   A soft metamorphic rock made up mostly of talc.

sod   Sections of the grass-covered surface of the ground.

taiga   Pine and birch forests.

tundra   A treeless plain that has black, mucky soil and a permanently frozen subsoil.

umiak   A boat covered with animal skins that can hold a small group of people.

warp   Stationary strands on a loom.

wattle and daub   A home-building method using woven saplings covered with mud.

weft   Strands that are woven into the warp.

*Knowledge learned is
knowledge gained.*

MARY WADE, MONACAN

Index